THE PROCESS

Level I

The Methodology, Philosophy & Principles of Coaching to Win

Developing the Holistic High School, College and Professional Team Sport Person

Fergus Connolly & Cameron Josse

1 Dedication

Cam

To Joe for always allowing me to thrive as an athlete and coach and to my beautiful wife Jen, for always being my light, my guide, my best friend and my angel.

1   DEDICATION   3

2   INTRODUCTION   13

2.1   THE EXPECTATION OF WINNING   15
2.1.1   MISSION: SUSTAINABLE SUCCESS   15

3   DEVELOPING A WINNING MODEL   19

3.1   START WITH THE GAME   19
3.2   THE LAWS OF THE GAME   19
3.2.1   THE LAW OF EXPECTED EMERGENCE   19
3.2.2   THE LAW OF INDIVIDUAL INFLUENCE   20
3.2.3   THE LAW OF TIME & SPACE   21
3.2.3.1   Technique Affects Space & Time   22
3.2.3.2   Effective Field Space   22
3.2.4   THE LAW OF BALL SPEED   23
3.2.4.1   Fast Ball   23
3.2.4.2   Slow Ball   24
3.2.4.3   Fast or Slow Ball?   25
3.2.5   THE LAW OF EXPOSURE   25
3.2.6   THE LAW OF OFFENSE   26
3.3   THE PARADOXES OF THE GAME   27
3.3.1   THE PARADOX OF POSSESSION & OPPORTUNITY   27
3.3.2   THE PARADOX OF FITNESS   28
3.3.2.1   The Object of the Game   30
3.3.3   THE PARADOX OF SPEED   30
3.3.3.1   Effective Speed   31
3.3.4   THE PARADOX OF INTENSITY   33
3.3.5   THE PARADOX OF INDIVIDUAL STATISTICS   33
3.3.6   THE PARADOX OF INJURY   34
3.3.7   THE PARADOX OF VICTORY   34
3.3.7.1   Covering All Bases   36

4   THE GAME MODEL   39

4.1   THE GLOBAL APPLICATION OF THE GAME MODEL   40
4.1.1   THE GAME MODEL FOR ALL COACHES   41

4.2 COMPREHENDING THE GAME MODEL   **41**

4.2.1   OFFENSIVE AND DEFENSIVE MOMENTS   42

4.2.2   TRANSITIONS IN FOOTBALL   42

4.2.3   THE GAME PRINCIPLES   43

4.2.3.1   Structure and Formation   44

4.2.3.2   Ball Movement   46

4.2.3.3   Player Movement   47

4.2.3.4   Player Relationships – Sequencing and Timing   48

4.3   MICRO-MOMENTS   **52**

4.3.1   WHY MICRO-MOMENTS?   52

4.3.2   OFFENSIVE PLAY MICRO MOMENTS   54

4.3.2.1   Construction – Create Usable Space   54

4.3.2.2   Penetration – Move into Opponent's Territory   54

4.3.2.3   Execution – Successfully Complete the Play   55

4.3.3   DEFENSIVE PLAY MICRO MOMENTS   55

4.3.3.1   Isolation – Close Down Space   55

4.3.3.2   Termination – Remove the Play Threat   55

4.3.3.3   Dispossession – Regain Possession of the Ball   56

4.3.4   TRANSITION FROM OFFENSE TO DEFENSE – GIVING UP TURNOVERS   56

4.3.4.1   Disrupt – Put Pressure on the Ball Carrier   57

4.3.4.2   Organize – Stay Fortified   57

4.3.4.3   Direct – Send the Ball Carrier Away from the End Zone   57

4.3.5   TRANSITION FROM DEFENSE TO OFFENSE – FORCING TURNOVERS   57

4.3.5.1   Movement – Move the Ball Quickly   58

4.3.5.2   Direction – Commit to an Immediate Path   58

4.3.5.3   Space – Find Room to Continue Movement   58

4.4   MACRO PRINCIPLES   **58**

4.4.1   MACRO PRINCIPLE OF OFFENSE – PLAYER SPACE   59

4.4.2   MACRO PRINCIPLE OF OFFENSE-TO-DEFENSE – BALL PRESSURE   59

4.4.3   MACRO PRINCIPLE OF DEFENSE – CONSTRAIN SPACE   59

4.4.4   MACRO PRINCIPLE OF DEFENSE-TO-OFFENSE – BALL SPEED   60

4.4.5   THE IMPORTANCE OF MACRO PRINCIPLES   60

4.5   MICRO PRINCIPLES   **61**

4.5.1   MICRO PRINCIPLES OF OFFENSIVE PLAY   61

4.5.1.1   Offensive Support – Create Big Play Opportunities   61

4.5.1.2   Width and Depth – Make the Field as Big as Possible   62

4.5.1.3   Balanced Offense – Use Multiple Attacking Options   63

4.5.1.4   Movement – Spread the Ball to Different Players   63

4.5.1.5   Misdirection –Hiding True Intentions   63

4.5.2   MICRO PRINCIPLES OF DEFENSIVE PLAY   64

4.5.2.1	Defensive Support – Do Your Job	64
4.5.2.2	Recovery – Take Back Momentum	64
4.5.2.3	Cover – Take Up Space	65
4.5.2.4	Balanced Defense – Hold Off Various Attacks	65
4.5.2.5	Compactness – Working to Prevent Penetration	65
4.6	**VISUALIZING THE GAME MODEL**	**66**
4.6.1	USING THE GAME MODEL TO IMPROVE PERFORMANCE	68
4.7	**BUILDING TEAM COHESION WITH COMMUNICATION**	**70**
4.7.1	DEVELOPING ORGANIZATIONAL FOCUS	71
4.7.2	AVOIDING CONFLICTING INTERESTS	72
4.7.3	FINDING SOLUTIONS, NOT DWELLING ON ERRORS	73
5	**PREPARING THE PLAYER**	**75**
5.1	**PEOPLE ARE CREATURES OF HABIT**	**75**
5.1.1	THE NEED FOR CONSISTENT ROUTINES	76
5.1.2	COMMUNICATION AND TEAM DYNAMICS	78
5.1.3	THE BIG PICTURE OF STRESS	78
5.2	**THE FOUR-COACTIVE MODEL OF PLAYER PREPARATION**	**80**
5.3	**THE TACTICAL COACTIVE**	**82**
5.3.1	TACTICAL CONTEXT AND MOMENTS	83
5.3.2	THE TACTICAL TO-DO LIST	84
5.3.3	GAME MODEL DRILL DESIGN	85
5.4	**THE TECHNICAL COACTIVE**	**86**
5.4.1	SPATIAL AWARENESS	86
5.4.2	FROM OBSERVATION TO ACTION	87
5.4.3	THE IMPORTANCE OF CONTEXT	90
5.4.4	THE LOCK AND THE KEY	91
5.4.5	TECHNICAL EXECUTION	92
5.4.6	TECHNICAL AND TACTICAL SYNERGY	93
5.5	**THE PSYCHOLOGICAL COACTIVE**	**93**
5.5.1	SPIRITUALITY	94
5.5.1.1	The Tribe	95
5.5.2	EMOTION	96
5.5.2.1	Out of Control	96
5.5.2.2	Emotional Intelligence	97
5.5.2.3	The Confidence Game	97
5.5.3	COGNITION	98
5.5.3.1	How Players Learn Best	98
5.5.3.2	Tapping into the Subconscious	99

5.5.3.3   Weekly Psychological Considerations   100
5.6   THE PHYSICAL COACTIVE   **101**
5.6.1   MOVEMENT AND MOTION   101
5.6.1.1   Biomechanics – Understanding Movement with Physics 101
5.6.1.2   Bioenergetics – Fueling Movement   108
5.6.2   ANTHROPOMETRICS – BODY SIZE, STRUCTURE, AND SHAPE   112
5.6.2.1   Body Structure & Biomechanics   112
5.6.3   DETERMINING LIMITING FACTORS   113
5.6.4   PHYSICAL PERFORMANCE QUALITIES   117
5.6.4.1   Energy System Performance Qualities   117
5.6.4.2   Neuromuscular Performance Qualities   120
5.6.4.3   Motor System Performance Qualities   120
5.6.5   THE MOST IMPORTANT FACTOR FOR SUSTAINABLE SUCCESS   123

6   PLAYER HEALTH   **125**

6.1   HEALTH, STRESS, AND PERFORMANCE   **125**
6.2   PSYCHO-PHYSIOLOGICAL HEALTH   **126**
6.2.1   HEALTH AND LONGEVITY   127
6.2.2   TRAINING SMARTER, NOT HARDER   127
6.3   THE PLAYER PERSONALITY   **129**
6.3.1   HIPPOCRATES, PSYCHOLOGY, AND PHYSIOLOGY   129
6.4   THE RESILIENT PLAYER   **130**

7   PREPARING THE TEAM   **133**

7.1   THE PROGRAMMING ELEMENTS   **133**
7.1.1   VOLUME   134
7.1.2   INTENSITY   134
7.1.3   DENSITY   135
7.1.4   COLLISION   135
7.2   WORKING BACKWARDS FROM THE GAME   **136**
7.2.1   RECOVERY RATES AND TRAINING RESIDUALS   136
7.2.2   THE GAME IS THE PRIMARY MEASURE OF PERFORMANCE   140
7.3   STRATEGIES FOR LEARNING SKILLS   **140**
7.3.1   VOLUME AND QUANTITY OF WORK   141
7.3.2   INTENSITY AND QUALITY OF TRAINING   141
7.3.3   DENSITY AND FREQUENCY OF TRAINING   141
7.3.4   COLLISION CONSIDERATIONS   142

7.4	PREPARING THE TEAM TO WIN GAMES	142
7.4.1	THE MORPHOCYCLE – MAXIMIZING EACH TRAINING WEEK	143
7.4.2	MORPHOCYCLE CONSIDERATIONS	146
7.4.2.1	The Three Phases of Team Preparation	146
7.4.2.2	Communicating with Principles	146
7.4.3	TACTICAL CONSIDERATIONS	148
7.4.4	TECHNICAL CONSIDERATIONS	148
7.4.4.1	The Test of Writing Your Name	149
7.4.4.2	Resiliency Over Robustness	150
7.4.4.3	Skill Specificity	150
7.4.4.4	Adding Perception	151
7.4.5	TECHNO-TACTICAL PREPARATION	151
7.4.6	PSYCHOLOGICAL CONSIDERATIONS	152
7.4.6.1	Emotional Considerations	152
7.4.6.2	Cognitive Considerations	153
7.4.6.3	Spiritual Considerations	154
7.4.6.4	What About Mental Toughness?	155
7.4.7	PHYSICAL CONSIDERATIONS	157
7.4.7.1	Weight Room Skill	157
8	**DESIGNING THE MORPHOCYCLE**	**161**
8.1	**BALANCING ELEMENTS OF THE MORPHOCYCLE**	**161**
8.1.1	DETERMINING & MANAGING GAME VOLUME	165
8.1.2	THE PRACTICE VOLUME PROBLEM	165
8.1.3	GAME VOLUME IS TEAM SPECIFIC	166
8.1.4	COMPETITION MODELING	166
8.1.5	THE TOTAL STRESS LOAD	169
8.2	**VOLUME EXPOSURE**	**171**
8.3	**INTENSITY EXPOSURE**	**171**
8.4	**DENSITY EXPOSURE**	**172**
8.5	**COLLISION EXPOSURE**	**173**
8.6	**SEQUENCING THE STIMULI**	**173**
8.7	**THE ANSWERS LIE IN HOUSE**	**174**
9	**USING GAMES TO PREPARE FOR GAMES**	**177**
9.1	**FROM PERCEPTION TO ACTION**	**178**
9.1.1	FACILITATING DECISION-MAKING	179

9.2	THE PHYSICAL BENEFITS OF TRAINING GAMES	180
9.3	MATCH UP GAMES	181
9.3.1	CLASSIFYING MATCH UP GAMES	183
9.4	MULTI-PLAYER GAMES	184
9.4.1	FORMATION-FOCUSED GAMES	185
9.4.2	SIMPLE INVASION GAMES	188
9.4.3	SMALL-SIDED GAMES	188
9.4.4	THE BASIS FOR ALL GAME INTELLIGENCE	190
9.4.5	MANIPULATING GAME RULES FOR DIFFERENT TRAINING EFFECTS	190
9.4.6	GENERAL GUIDELINES FOR TRAINING GAMES	194
9.4.7	PLACING GAMES IN THE WORKOUT TEMPLATE	195

10	WINNING AND LEADERSHIP	199

10.1	THE SIX LAWS OF WINNING	199
10.1.1	THE LAW OF KNOWLEDGE	199
10.1.2	THE LAW OF HUMAN SUPERIORITY	199
10.1.3	THE LAW OF INTENSITY AND QUALITY	200
10.1.4	THE LAW OF INDIVIDUAL CONTRIBUTION	201
10.1.5	THE LAW OF PREPARATION	201
10.1.6	THE LAW OF SUPPORT	202
10.2	THE FOUR PRIMARY PRINCIPLES OF WINNING TEAMS	203
10.2.1	HUMILITY	203
10.2.2	HUNGER	205
10.2.2.1	Accountability	205
10.2.2.2	Focus	205
10.2.3	HARD WORK	206
10.2.3.1	Commitment	207
10.2.4	HONESTY	207

11	CONCLUSION	211

12	AUTHORS	212

13	ONLINE EDUCATION	214

14	GAME CHANGER	215

15	COMING SOON	216
17	59 LESSONS	217
18	SUGGESTED READING	218
19	NOTES	220

2 Introduction

Football Sunday. America's unofficial holiday. For anyone living in the United States, it is known all too well the impact that this game has on American culture. Ask most people and they will tell you - during football season, the National Football League (NFL) owns Sundays.

America's game has remained a staple event of Sunday life for most families for the past 30 years. Although its place has remained constant in American culture off the field, the game is constantly evolving. It has moved from pro-style schemes to the West Coast offense, from the 4-3 defense to the 3-4 scheme, with a seemingly endless list of rule changes that take place every year. Over the past 10 years, coaching the game has also changed – but not in ways that have necessarily helped.

Teams have been forming larger coaching staffs, adding more assistants, fostering sports science departments, advancing strength & conditioning programs and generating larger rosters. But at this point, it's hard to say if any of these factors have led to dramatic improvements in team performances. In fact, in many cases these changes have caused more problems, more confusion, and have led to disjointed programs and inconsistent results.

A common major drawback to the rise of different departments is the absence of a cohesive philosophy shared throughout the organization. This results in isolated silos of staff members who fail to communicate properly. This silo structure leads many to misinterpret player and/or coaching needs and engage in poor roster management.

As an example, the absence of a clear, unified model, combining coaching tactics with physical preparation, can lead to strength & conditioning practices that operate without a clear understanding of what coaches want to see on game day. In effect, the preparation programs are not tailored to help players achieve what the playbook requires.

In addition, if there is no weekly training schedule in place to optimize recovery, rehabilitation and nutrition, keeping these factors in line with the daily emphasis of practice, players may be overstressed and not perform at their best on game day.

As a final example, when teams/organizations operate without a unifying model, it becomes progressively harder to lead from a coaching perspective. In football, the head coach is the captain of the ship, and his vision is the path that the whole team must take together.

Consequently, if there is no team-wide model to support a coach's vision, sustaining success will become troublesome. In order to effectively lead, there must first exist some understanding of how people operate, both mentally and physically. Then, formulation of an organizational model can support this understanding and help put a team on the road to sustainable success.

Based on the ideas proposed in "*Game Changer – The Art of Sports Science*" by Fergus Connolly, we present here, for the first time, an approach that eliminates these issues in coaching, from the top down. Simply put, our objective is to share a clear philosophy with one single aim - to win games.

This is the first installment in a series that will dive deeper into understanding how a common communication system can lay the foundation for a championship program. The principles associated with this philosophy are *universal* team sports principles. They are not exact prescriptions or hand-out answers. Instead, they are common denominators of how high-level programs operate in all team sports.

The objectives of this philosophy are to:
- Develop the life skills young men need to be successful as members of society.
- Win as many games as possible.
- Play the game to the highest ability.
- Build a sustainable organization that develops players and coaches for the long term.

"The flexibility of being able to learn from others and change what you do relative to how the game changes is very, very important."

- Nick Saban

2.1   The Expectation of Winning

The obvious goal of any team is to win games. The desire to win is one of the most admirable qualities in any human endeavor. But, where sport stands right now, coaches have more than just a *desire* to win - they face a *necessity* to win, or risk losing their livelihoods.

> *The desire to win is one of the most admirable*
> *qualities in any human endeavor.*

Head coaches, athletic directors and general managers have been trying to crack the "winning code" ever since the inception of sport. Fans and supporters *expect* their teams to do well and win games. As a result, in both collegiate and professional settings, head coaches have small windows of opportunity to find success.

In today's competitive world, coaches have less and less time to get results. Coaches might start sacrificing what they know to be winning principles in exchange for achieving instant results. Maybe they forego the plan to gradually build a team of young players, and instead opt for transfers or free agent players who promise to be productive from the get-go.

The pressure is real. It's not uncommon for some coaches to have only two years to turn a program around. As a result, organizations spend vast sums of money on specialists and additional staff members with the goal of solving problems and winning games immediately. Despite this effort, many teams still fail.

2.1.1   Mission: Sustainable Success

Long-term development of players is rare at any level of sport, largely due to the constant pressure for instant success. Even high school coaches are consistently on the hot seat if they don't win games. Still, one of the greatest detriments to an organization is the absence of a definitive plan or system by which to analyze how a team is performing. Organizations struggle to identify areas where problems might exist and how to solve them.

Many are familiar with the "silo" structure that is currently under scrutiny in business and sport. Too often, departments work independently rather than *inter-dependently* – separately rather than together. Such silos lead to conflicting communications among team members and staff, contributing to a misalignment of resources and under-performance.

Consider this book series our attempt to help teams get back on track to winning games and forging dynasties. It is by no means a perfect solution and might not be applicable to all coaches or all teams. It is simply our understanding of what can help a team become better organized, based on our experience of working and communicating with those who have found success at the highest levels of business and sport.

3 Developing a Winning Model

If there is any real hope of producing a sustainable, winning program, the first step must be creating a blueprint that serves everyone involved - from the grounds-man to the head coach, to the athletic director or general manager. This blueprint helps everyone understand the game in a digestible way and allows for efficient and effective job performances in cohesion with all other staff members. The real goal here is communication, cohesion, and alignment.

3.1 Start with the Game

This blueprint starts at the level of the game and works backward to determine how best to prepare. If everyone understands exactly what is expected of the team on game day, then the destination is clear. This blueprint is referred to as a Game Model, which will be covered shortly.

3.2 The Laws of the Game

Before reviewing the Game Model, one must first acknowledge and accept the "laws" of the game. As Fergus outlined in *Game Changer*, these laws are universal to all team sports. Comprehending these basic laws is critical to developing a productive Game Model and winning games.

3.2.1 The Law of Expected Emergence

High level performers will execute based on the instincts they've developed and their ability to anticipate what's about to happen.

In high pressure situations, actions are dictated by habit. While a situation may occasionally appear as new, nothing (in principle) should happen on a game field that has not been prepared for in some way. The principles of the game and the associated moments and sequences should be so ingrained in players that they develop a heightened game intelligence, allowing them to respond to fluctuations and chaos.

*High level performers will execute based on the
instincts they've developed and their ability to
anticipate what's about to happen.*

Success in sport is dependent on the ability to execute skills in a chaotic environment against a well-prepared opponent. All coaches and players watch film and scout each other, so there will always be an understanding of what an opponent is likely to do and what must be done to counter it. In other words, there are no real secrets, especially when teams face each other more than once per season.

The goal is to do what has been repeatedly done before, but to do it faster and better than the opponent. If this "simple" task can be accomplished, it will be a struggle for any opponent to force a team to yield. The opponent might know exactly what is about to happen but will have limited success in stopping it from happening.

3.2.2   The Law of Individual Influence

Teams will always have influential players who are simply better than everyone else on the team.

As most coaches understand, not all players are created equal and some have more influence on the outcome of a game than others. If this wasn't true, then every starting player in college football would be an NFL draft pick and every NFL starter would be an All-Pro player.

*Some players have more influence on the outcome
of a game than others*

Thus, reducing the impact of influential players on opposing teams is paramount to winning. These influential players can significantly alter the state of the game, and they have an unequal influence on the game result.
A team's most influential players must stay healthy and remain on the field to have great success. Moreover, it is also a team's responsibility to develop all players on the roster to maximize their potential for influence.

"He's smart, he's explosive, he's competitive, he's giving effort every single play and he's powerful. So, the guy has no weaknesses and that's a frustrating thing for an offensive lineman to go up against."[*]

– Offensive lineman Jason Kelce, describing defensive lineman Aaron Donald

3.2.3   The Law of Time & Space

Space creates time, but time cannot always create space.

What is perceived as having a lot of time on the field means having a lot of space. When quarterbacks are described as having "all day" to throw the football, the offensive line is giving the quarterback enough space to operate and find a receiver down field.

Space creates time, but time cannot always create space.

In order to create space in one area, space must be compressed somewhere else. Offenses compress defenders with physical force by blocking, pass the ball to different areas of the field, or use misdirection and/or play action to freeze opponents in place. This is the key to creating vertical and horizontal stretches on the field.

The football field is 120 yards long, including the depth of the end zones, and 53 1/3 yards wide. A critical aspect of success on any play is the creation or compression of space within this physical boundary. The law of space tells us that if space does not exist in one area, it must exist in another.

Game rules and tactics certainly have an influence over space manipulation. In football, the offense can create up to eight gaps of space for a ball carrier in the run game by manipulating the movement of the line of scrimmage and can attack nine pass zones in the passing game. As a result, the opposing defense must find a scheme that allows eleven defenders to adequately cover those areas of space.

3.2.3.1   Technique Affects Space & Time

The best offensive football players always appear to have more time than everyone else and this is the result of their ability to create space. For ball carriers, creating space could be as simple as a head fake or side-step. Their superior technical ability and skill allows them to create space in two ways:

First, they will be more biomechanically efficient than their opponents, meaning they will be able to move faster and with less effort and stress. Second, superior players are exceptional at altering or disabling opponents' decision-making cycle, forcing them to become self-conscious and freeze.

> *Better players create space through great technique.*

Creating space is about more than just sprinting speed. In fact, pure movement speed is often *not* the determining factor of successful execution for elite players. Players can use technique to execute effectively even when they have started slowing down later in their careers. Older players use experience to compensate when they can no longer rely on their physical gifts. Coaches can also use tactical strategy to create space through mismatches, formations, or play calling. The goal of creating space is to create more time to act.

3.2.3.2   Effective Field Space

Creating space is about maximizing the amount of the field that is usable for moving the ball. This is understood as *effective field space*. Different formations and player movement strategies can be used on offense to create more effective field space. This explains how offenses can create space into the boundary where it may seem that not much physical space is available. If there is a lane for the ball carrier to run through, there is effective field space.

> *"We always talk about using all five eligibles - spreading the field, making sure that everybody has got to be accounted for."[viii]*
>
> *- Los Angeles Rams head coach Sean McVay*

Naturally, if the offensive goal is to create as much usable space as possible then the defensive goal is to limit the effective field space by restricting movement and closing off lanes.

3.2.4   The Law of Ball Speed

The complexity and rate of all decision-making in the game are determined by ball speed, not player speed.

Ball speed encompasses how quickly the ball is lined up, snapped, and transported to a ball carrier over the course of a drive and throughout the game. The slower the ball speed, the greater the cognitive processing time for opponents, giving them more time to react.

> *Ball speed determines the complexity and rate of decision-making in the game.*

Why would the ball be the deciding factor of how fast the game moves?
The ball is the key target during any play and its movement will determine the tempo of all actions and decision-making.

For example, if an offense uses a slow-tempo, huddle-based offense, then the defense will have to match this tempo. The same phenomenon occurs if an offense is running a no-huddle, up-tempo offense with minimal rest and very fast ball movement. It's not a purely physical phenomenon, but a cognitive one as well. A team's decision to use aspects of fast or slow ball will help determine the rhythm established throughout the game.

3.2.4.1   Fast Ball

Simply put, fast ball refers to fast game play. When Chip Kelly took over as head coach at the University of Oregon, the college football world was amazed by how fast his players were able to line up, snap the ball, exploit the opposition, and score lots of points. The sudden increase in the speed of decision-making was what caused the greatest trouble for opposing teams.

Many schools adopted a similar philosophy in hopes of replicating similar results. But as one might expect, adopting a philosophy only works when the roster is properly suited for it and everyone is on the same page. This is a reason for using a Game Model approach.

One might assume it is physically tiring for an offense to play at a consistently high tempo, but the truth is that players can quickly adopt the necessary fitness and mental resilience necessary to withstand the tactical speed when the Game Model is clear, understood, and practiced. When players understand the Game Model well, they will adapt to the tempo at a much faster rate. As a result, players will execute effectively, and the opposing defense will be worn down physically and mentally as their defensive Game Plan is disrupted.

Fast ball can benefit many offensive teams. Ironically, although fast ball increases the complexity of the game, this approach can be very successful for lower-skilled teams. Fast ball requires young players to make instinctive, subconscious decisions, because the ball moves too fast and they are less likely to over think. But of course, highly skilled players who can play at a fast tempo are much more threatening.

3.2.4.2   Slow Ball

Traditional pro-style offenses will often huddle and take up most of the time on the play clock before initiating the next snap of the ball. In these schemes, teams call fewer total plays in comparison to fast ball schemes. However, due to the longer time of possession, the cognitive and technical abilities of the defensive players are challenged.

More time means there is more time to (over)think and less reliance on instinct and habit. Defensive players might find themselves becoming more self-conscious when the time between plays increases. Since more time is available between plays, the offensive players have more time to recover and operate at faster playing speeds. This means that one wrong move by the defense could prove catastrophic and lead to a big play at any moment.

From the other vantage point, the offensive players also need be aware that the defensive players will be better rested and operating faster as well, so blockers must be able to fit their blocks accordingly and receivers must run the correct routes on pass plays. When compared to a fast tempo, there won't be as much ability to catch the defense off balance, so execution becomes increasingly important.

3.2.4.3   Fast or Slow Ball?

The most robust teams can deploy aspects of both fast and slow ball. The New England Patriots are a great example of a team that can quickly shift into a hurry-up, no-huddle offense, then suddenly slow the game down, line up in a power formation, and try to smash the ball forward. Thus, the teams with the best tempo are teams that can change their pace to fit the context of what they want to accomplish and the feedback the defense is providing.

> *"Tempo is more important than total speed, and the ability to manage 'game tempo' comes with experience."*
>
> *-Mike Comberds, Complementary Football Concept*

Once again, there are many factors involved in deciding a team's playing style. Bigger players will often find that playing at a faster tempo is more physically demanding. But the suitability of ball speed and the approach a head coach takes to his tactical design are usually determined by the players available. The scheme must suit the people on the team.

3.2.5   The Law of Exposure

The players and teams exposed to the highest game speeds and situational complexities are those who can execute the best under pressure.

The best teams execute big plays and make incredible decisions on the largest stages. Players have described daily practices at the University of Alabama under coach Nick Saban as feeling like games. If a team recruits and signs many of the nation's best prospects and demands game-like speed and decision-making daily in practice, the result is a recipe for five national championships since 2009."

While the stress load imposed on players must certainly be monitored, exposure to game-like intensities and learning situations that represent game elements are necessary for players to continue finding solutions to problems of rising complexity. As will be covered in greater detail later, in order to consistently practice at game-like intensity a corresponding emphasis must be placed on rest and recovery, or players will quickly be run into the ground.

> *Players and teams most frequently exposed to the highest speeds of play and game complexity are those that can execute the best under pressure.*

Antonio Brown, unquestionably one of the most productive NFL wide receivers, consistently lines up against the league's best defensive backs and finds ways to succeed, even when the odds seem stacked against him. When teams put their best defensive backs on Brown, they are also giving him opportunities to develop against the highest level of competition. As a result, Brown almost always finds a way to stay one step ahead of defensive backs in the NFL.

Teams who play against proven opponents like the Alabama Crimson Tide or New England Patriots will naturally raise their game intensity to rise to the challenge. Of course, this also gives those great teams constant and valuable exposure to demanding scenarios.

3.2.6   The Law of Offense

For successful teams, a *pro*-active mindset is utilized rather than a *re*-active mindset.

This is present in all team sports, not just football. What this means is that the mindset is always to attack. A team either has possession of the ball or is attacking the opponent to regain possession of the ball.

> *There is no such thing as defense, only offense without the ball.*

Teams should always be proactive and take the initiative. The goal is to keep the opposing players "on their heels." If a team loses the ability to be proactive, it resorts to acting on the opponent's wishes and chances of winning drastically drop. Developing an attacking mindset even for defensive players to win the ball back, rather than simply to defend the field, is paramount to keeping an entire team proactive.

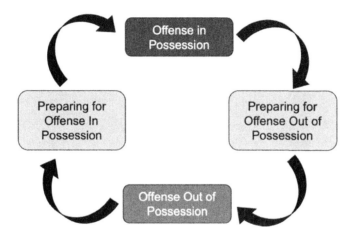

3.3 The Paradoxes of the Game

In addition to the laws of the game, there are some common paradoxes and fallacies associated with sport. These are important to consider so that one does not lose track of what's important when assessing team performance. These paradoxes, such as "the fittest team always wins," have become accepted by many without any critical analysis. In this section, some of these common claims are challenged by staying true to the context of the game.

3.3.1 The Paradox of Possession & Opportunity

It is a common misconception that the team with the most time of possession will always be the victor. Time of possession will surely provide better chances at having opportunities to score, but it really comes down to effectiveness versus efficiency.

A team might be efficient enough to keep the ball moving but if the drive stalls without any points (especially touchdowns), how effective was it?

Teams with less coherence will struggle to be effective.

Teams that have more experience together will find ways to score more often, due to the cohesion among the players and coaches. Practice sessions and drills that represent game situations can be invaluable for a team to develop the cohesion needed to score as much as possible. The tactics designed by the coaching staff must be matched with the strengths of a team as it currently stands which can change from week to week.

Statistics like passing yards, rushing yards, tackles, or sacks mean little if they are not directly contributing to team effectiveness. The statistics analyzed and used as a team's key performance indicators (KPI's) - the data that helps determine the success of the Game Plan - must accurately tell the story of the game and reflect the key moments on the field that determined the outcome. In other words, a staff should ask, "How do the stats help us determine if the Game Plan was effective?"

Gaining lots of offensive yards is great, but did the team set up any scoring opportunities? When scoring opportunities were present, was the team able to execute and change the scoreboard? The intent is to win games. So, the KPI's that are chosen must truly reflect and evaluate the outcome of the game, which many "fluff" statistics do not.

3.3.2   The Paradox of Fitness

A common traditional mindset is that if players are not performing well in games, it's because they are "out of shape." As a result, more running might be added at the end of practice or the strength and conditioning coaches might be instructed to raise the intensity of player workouts.

*The only data that truly matters is whether the players
executed their playbook responsibilities as well as
possible in practice and games.*

What must be thoroughly understood is the context of the game and how players play the game. Fitness is certainly important, but there are more factors to consider when it comes to player performance and winning games. Players must be fit enough to play and stay healthy but ultimately it is their technical skill, tactical awareness and mental health that determine whether they put their physical fitness into action and execute effectively. Legendary Stanford and San Francisco coach Bill Walsh believed that player success extends far beyond the level of physical fitness:

*"Physical strength and speed are important advantages,
but even more advantageous is having the training that
permits us to respond intelligently to whatever confronts
us. That means more precision, better execution and
quicker responses than our opponents. Under the
extreme stress of game conditions, a player must
condense his intellect and focus it on thinking more
quickly and clearly than the opposition."*

- Bill Walsh

In terms of game-day performance, the amount of linear running a player does while conditioning is largely irrelevant. Of course, the game necessitates a baseline fitness requirement; however, players will move based on the requirements of the task and in response to their environments.

If players can accomplish their sport task using less total energy and covering less distance, we cannot be upset if data from global positioning systems (GPS) show less distance covered than we expected. Sports science data works best as a system of checks and balances, not as a complete governor of how training is performed. The only data that truly matters is whether players execute their playbook responsibilities as well as possible in practice and games. A wide receiver that runs harder than the others but drops seven out of ten passes is of little use to us on game day.

3.3.2.1   The Object of the Game

A team of smart, prepared players does not run the most. Rather, these players force opponents to run more and conserve their energy for when it really counts. By using effective formations, player movement, ball movement, timing, and sequencing, coaches can keep players feeling fresh and playing effectively while wearing down the opponent physically and mentally.

However, the volume of running might rise considerably due to the movement of the ball. Therefore, ball speed, not player speed, determines how the game is played. One week a team might play an opponent that uses a slow style of offense and the players don't run very much. Then the very next week it might play a fast ball team and run a lot more.

This is where realistic practice scenarios are vital, so coaches can adjust the Game Plan to account for the upcoming opponent's style of play. If players understand what it takes to execute effectively, based on the principles of the Game Model, the movement solutions will manifest accordingly.

3.3.3   The Paradox of Speed

Coaches frequently utter the phrase "speed kills." If they aren't obsessed with conditioning, then they are certainly obsessed with speed. The obsession is typically based on players' 40-yard dash times. A player might be labeled as "a 4.3 guy" or something similar and this immediately impacts how scouts might value that player.

But the 40-yard dash is just a linear sprinting test performed while wearing compression gear – without any opponents – and is based on how quickly players can cover 40 yards while employing their own starting action. If context is truly king, then one can easily understand how this test has little relevance to actual game situations. In a football game, speed must be applied in full pads while maneuvering around opponents and other obstacles. Game-oriented speed is based upon *optimal* movement that achieves tactical goals in response to environmental constraints.

Frank Gore is a great example of a running back who has had a long career due to his decision-making and his ability to run at the appropriate speed for the situations in front of him. His perceptual abilities – how fast his brain processes information for action – are fast enough that he can still be effective even if he is "slower" on paper than other running backs.

3.3.3.1 Effective Speed

Obviously, speed is important. Players capable of achieving higher top speeds will have a higher **speed reserve**, meaning they will be able to operate faster at any level of effort. To explain further, if two different players are asked to make the exact same play, a faster player might only need to use 70 percent of his maximum effort to be successful, while a slower player might need to use 90 percent. In other words, one player's 70 percent is another player's 90 percent, even though the absolute speed being displayed is the same.

The trick lies in how effectively speed can be applied. If a running back starts turning on the jets but can't decelerate enough to make it around the last defender, then he might miss an opportunity to evade an opponent and score a touchdown. The same goes for a defensive back who starts sprinting full speed to keep up with what he thinks is a deep route by the receiver, only to find himself out of place when the receiver decelerates and redirects into a comeback route.

Speed is a physical output that must be combined with perceptual-cognitive abilities in order to be effective on game day. Many players are described as "slow" based on their 40-yard dash times, but their understanding of the game and their technique help them play very fast.

A great example is wide receiver Cooper Kupp who ran a 4.62 40-yard dash at the 2017 NFL Combine. Scouts consider this a "slow" time for a wide receiver. But if scouts put on his game film, they quickly realize that he plays with the necessary speed to be effective. The Los Angeles Rams realized this and drafted him in the third round of the 2017 NFL Draft. They evaluated correctly. Kupp was productive as a rookie, totaling 62 receptions for 869 yards and five touchdowns, while averaging 14 yards per catch in 15 games.

"I think our offense has become predicated on what our players do well. It's not rigid, where we have to have this, or we have to have that. We've had tall receivers. We've had short receivers. We've had fast ones. We've had slower ones. We've had big linemen, smaller linemen. Big tight ends, blocking tight ends. Small backs, big backs. What we do here is try to find good football players, get them on our roster, and try to let them do what they do well."

- Josh McDaniels, New England Patriots Offensive Coordinator

3.3.3.1.1   Optimal Movement Speed

Caution must be taken when telling players to move at full speed. When looking honestly at what really happens in the game, the expectation that players should consistently hit maximum running speeds is a complete falsehood. It's easy to critique player speeds now that movement-tracking technology and other similar forms of sports science are readily available. Consequently, one can easily be misled by comparing game-based movement speeds to linear speed tests like the 40-yard dash.

There is a huge difference between what a player does in a 40-yard dash and what he does in a game. A 40-yard dash is performed in the absence of an opponent, engages far fewer sensory inputs to the environment, and does not require significant cognitive recall. Instead, it's more productive to encourage players to play at their **optimal speed** – that is, the maximum speed at which they can move with proper technique in a game scenario while adhering to their tactical assignment.

The irony is that players who strive to run as fast as they can often end up losing control and being scolded for "trying to do too much." This is seen when pass rushers miss a sack, receivers take their eyes off the ball and drop a catch, or a safety misses a tackle after falling for a fake.

The emphasis should remain on maximizing game performance, rather than moving at maximum speed or cornering an assessment towards any other physical trait in isolation. With proper focus and development in a game context, the players will understand the relationships between their teammates and opponents so that they can do as much as necessary to do their jobs properly.

3.3.4   The Paradox of Intensity

Game intensity is based upon a combination of physical outputs, psychological state, technical skill, and tactical knowledge. Players must understand how to take advantage of their **functional reserve** – that is, their total available energy for playing over the course of a practice or game.

Functional reserve is based on more than what players are doing physically. As the game goes on, energy is drained by mental and emotional factors as well. Players (and coaches, through use of substitutions) must manage the intensity and effort as much as possible while keeping the big picture in mind - winning the game.

3.3.5   The Paradox of Individual Statistics

The fundamental goal of defenders is to bring down the ball carrier. But simply having a high number of tackles or sacks can be misleading in the context of winning a game.

For example, it might be the duty of a defensive player *not* to tackle, but instead make sure that space is constrained so that the ball carrier has nowhere to run and will be taken down by teammates. This is common for edge players like defensive ends, outside linebackers, or cornerbacks who must "set the edge" or "contain" the ball from traveling outside. By doing so, the interior players can pursue from the inside out and make sure the ball carrier is tackled.

In the NFL, pass rushers literally make their money by pressuring the quarterback. But pass rushers can obsess over sack numbers and become self-serving and damaging to the team. Consider a defensive end who knows he will get paid, drafted, or recruited if he can get sacks and therefore decides that he will only give effort in passing situations. If the offense is in a run situation, this player might not show much motivation to do his job. Suddenly, on third and long, it's as if he transforms into a different person so he can get the sack. But by taking plays off during normal yardage situations, he is hurting the productivity of the defensive unit.

Theoretically, if an NFL pass rusher gets just one sack in every regular season game, he would finish with 16 sacks and be recognized as one of the league's best. So, if this player manages to get a sack in the first quarter of the game, will he stay mentally engaged for the next three quarters? One player having a great statistical season tells nothing about how well the team is performing.

Statistics in isolation don't paint a complete picture

Players should be reminded that if they succeed together, they also succeed individually. A successful team creates the perception that all its players are dominant. The New England Patriots have put different players on the field year after year and haven't had a losing record since 2000. Individual statistics are minimally important to the broad picture of successful team play.

3.3.6   The Paradox of Injury
While most people would agree that it's important to keep *all* players as healthy as possible, a reality of sport is the necessity of keeping the most influential players on the field. If a team has a dominant quarterback who goes down for the rest of the season with an injury and his backup is far less adequate, the team will risk losing games. On the other hand, if the third string quarterback gets hurt in practice, the team will likely continue onward without taking any steps back.

3.3.7   The Paradox of Victory
How can a team defeat an opponent? Is it because the players are better conditioned? Perhaps. If so, then give a nice pat on the back to the strength and conditioning staff. This can certainly happen at the high school level, where players are still experiencing significant physical development. But this is rarely the case in college or the NFL, where most teams are in very similar physical shape. Victory is attributed to having better players, better learning experiences in practice, better decision-making skills, and better execution.

*Victor's bias can allow for faulty explanations of why a
team won*

When a team wins a game, a phenomenon known as **victor's bias** impacts the winning team, the losing team, and all the spectators who witnessed the game. Victor's bias basically allows for faulty explanations of why a team won a game, such as "our team is in better shape than yours" or "we have more skilled players than you do."

This presents two major challenges. If a team wins, it is important to manage expectations and have enough humility to keep the focus on continued improvement. Ignoring the score after the game is the only way to do this. Even if a team blows out an opponent by 40 points, it must acknowledge its mistakes.

When a team loses a game, the score and the associated emotions must be removed from the critical analysis. If that does not occur, the team will fail to recognize why the game was lost and risk failing to properly scout the upcoming opponent. Nick Saban summed up "victor's bias" perfectly:

*"It's not human nature to be great. It's human nature to
survive, to be average and do what we have to do to get
by. That is normal. When we have something good
happen, it's the special people that can stay focused and
keep paying attention to detail, working to get better and
not being satisfied with what they have accomplished."*

- Nick Saban

Player technical skill and tactical understanding of the game are hugely important for winning, especially in games that are decided in the fourth quarter. Players who are best prepared technically and tactically are the players able to maintain the most focus. These players don't get mentally beaten down and remain focused on what they need to do and when they need to do it.

The coaches that make the best in-game tactical decisions are those who control their emotions and understand the job at hand. Time spent arguing an irreversible call with an official can be time spent deciding how best to proceed from the current situation and get the Game Plan back on track.

Having a successful team is less about having the most "freakish" players on the roster and more about having players that display superior technical skill and tactical awareness. This is especially true in the NFL, where every player was cherry-picked from the best selection of college football players and all have similar physical abilities. We cannot assume that a team loses simply because it is not strong enough, fast enough, or "in shape" enough. The picture is far broader than that.

3.3.7.1   Covering All Bases

When a team loses, it must analyze subjective and objective markers that determine why players were unable to perform well enough to win. From a physical standpoint, the most important quality is that players are fit enough to play the game. If they are, then other issues are at stake. These other issues could include the need for developing leadership to boost psychological well-being, improving player decision-making, or progressing player skill through realistic learning experiences.

Just because a team is very fit does not mean players are prepared to work together and win a game. To go a step further, falsely assuming players are *not* fit enough can easily lead a team down the road to overtraining and possible injury from excessive practice and workouts.

A solid Game Model allows a team to correctly analyze and understand why a game was won or lost and adjustments can be made as the season progresses. This can include making more informed decisions about the focus of individual and team periods so that errors are corrected, and weaknesses are alleviated while keeping the overall objectives in place.

4 The Game Model

The Game Model is a coach's way of explaining and understanding the game. It is a simplified, principled approach, but it is the "model" that is used to "explain" the game.

The Game Model is a tool used by everyone in an organization to communicate in one common language. The Game Model represents the idea of how the game is played and outlines the different moments of the game in ways that are accepted and understood by the coaching staff, support staff, and players.

The Game Model is not a Game Plan or playbook. While the Game Plan will outline the specific strategies and tactics that coexist with the Game Model, a detailed Game Model, by its nature, influences *all* areas of performance – everything from the playbook to strength and conditioning and recruiting/scouting.

The Game Model ensures that the staff members associated with physical training, rehabilitation, recruiting/scouting, nutrition, sports psychology, and any other special areas understand the big picture. Everything is related to and communicated through the "model." Therefore, the Game Model exists at a level above the playbook. It is an organization-wide philosophy of understanding the game. Using this approach as the starting point allows a team to avoid operating with misaligned intentions.

Coaches can change how they choose to play the game, but they can't change the game itself. The Game Model is used as a blueprint to better understand the game so a team can design tactics and strategies to be successful within its boundaries. The goal of the Game Model is to find the best way to explain the game, keeping everyone on the same page with consistent communication.

The goal of the Game Model is to find the best way to explain the game.

Since the Game Model is primarily used for education and understanding, it's okay for the teaching points of the model to be challenged, refined and developed while keeping the most obvious team goal in mind – winning more games. A coaching staff that works together with trust, honesty and humility is better able to identify the limiting factors of the team so that the Game Model principles can form and fall into their rightful place, giving the team the best chance of success.

While it might sound as though a Game Model changes all the time, nothing could be further from the truth. The model itself serves as a blueprint of principles that the coaches and players are expected to adhere to over the course of a sustainable period. Once an organization adopts the principles, they should remain intact. While the way these principles are communicated might change, perhaps to make them simpler and more understandable, the principles themselves should stay consistent.

Elements of communicating a sound Game Model include:
- A dynamic, living and evolving idea.
- A description of team identity on game day.
- A collection of identifiable and distinguishable principles.
- Always open-ended, allowing answers to be found in-house as a team.

4.1   The Global Application of the Game Model

The principles of the Game Model do not change. Only the application of these principles can change. For example, the Macro Principle of Offensive Play is to create space for anyone who has or will receive possession of the ball. This principle belongs to the Game Model, since it cannot be changed – if an offense does not create space for the ball carrier, there will be no way to advance the ball or score points. But this principle must be understood and communicated to the players.

Consider a wide receiver who does not fully understand this principle. He may not comprehend the dire necessity of giving full effort in blocking to provide space for the ball carrier. It's not enough just to tell a wide receiver to block someone – he must understand the principle of creating space and the major negative impact when he does not do his job.

Whether running or passing the ball, creating space is the Macro Principle of Offensive Play and must be deeply understood by all offensive players. A sound comprehension of the Game Model will communicate this principle and foster that understanding.

4.1.1   The Game Model for All Coaches

The strength & conditioning staff can design games and activities during offseason training that put players in situations where they must create space in order to be successful. These do not have to be football-specific games. In fact, all field-based team sports operate under the same basic principles. So, any time players are in an offensive situation trying to score in the opponent's territory, they must create space.

Players cannot be expected to learn these principles or physically perform them unless they are physically and psychologically healthy. This is where the Game Model affects the rehabilitation staff, medical team, nutrition staff, sports psychology staff, and anyone else who has a hand in keeping players healthy.

Unhealthy players will not be able to help a team in the long run. When an organization's medical personnel understand how players are expected to perform from a physical, cognitive, and psychological standpoint, then the team is already on a faster track to keeping players healthy and winning games.

4.2   Comprehending the Game Model

Effective organizations must present and explain the Game Model to their support staff personnel. An easy start is going over the **Game Moments** – offense, defense, the transition from offense to defense, and the transition from defense to offense.

However, the two primary moments are offense and defense. At any moment in the game a team is either attacking with the ball or attacking without it. Players are either trying to score or prevent scoring, regardless of whether base personnel or special teams are on the field.

Within each Game Moment there are Micro Moments that underpin how game events unfold. Lastly, over-arching **Game Principles** are constantly present and the team that best adheres to these principles will almost always be the victor.

4.2.1   Offensive and Defensive Moments

In general, the moments of the game can be divided into aspects of **Offensive Play** and **Defensive Play.** The former includes any situation where scoring becomes the prerogative and the latter describes the situations where a team wants to prevent scoring at all costs. Special teams also fall into these categories. For example, kickoff coverage is a moment of Defensive Play and kickoff return is a moment of Offensive Play.

The advantage of using this approach is recognizing that the rules and objectives are universal and specific to the moment – not the personnel. With this, a team can find a more accurate interpretation and segmentation of technical and physical metrics used in sports science.   This framework can be used to start applying context to data and finding ways to truly affect the game result.

For experienced coaches, breaking the game down this way is certainly not news. However, each moment must be understood as having equal contribution to the success of a team. Of course, compensations are always present. A team could have a tremendous offense but give up a lot of points on defense and vice versa. A team might also be great on offense and defense but struggle on special teams, allowing a kick return for a touchdown, or losing field position after a blocked punt. But, if the intent of the coaching staff is to teach players to treat all Game Moments with importance, the chances of team success increase instantly.

4.2.2   Transitions in Football

In football, transitions from offense to defense or vice versa are not as common as other team sports but they are critical, nonetheless. For purposes of simplicity, turnovers can be considered as moments of transition. If the ball instantly changes possession on an interception or fumble recovery, then that moment becomes a transitional moment as teams suddenly switch roles.

One can argue that transitions also occur on special teams like kickoffs and punts, where one team delivers possession to the other team. While this is true, the broad principles and Game Moments governing these events are the same as what is found on offense or defense. Turnovers exist in a class of their own due to the immediate shock and rapid-fire response time needed by both teams in highly chaotic moments.

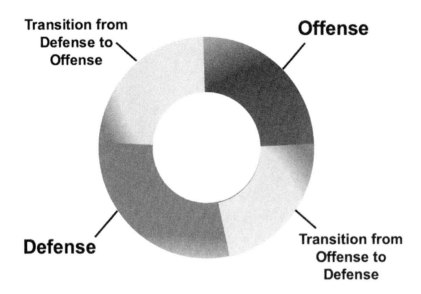

4.2.3   The Game Principles

The Game Principles are global, regardless of the specific Game Moment. This means that whether a team is on offense, defense, or special teams, the exact same over-arching principles apply. In *Game Changer,* Fergus explains and demonstrates how these principles are found in every team sport, on every team, with every player, regardless of the specific schemes, tactics, or strategies being employed.

There are four Game Principles:

1. Structure and Formation
2. Ball Movement
3. Player Movement
4. Player Sequencing/Timing of Actions

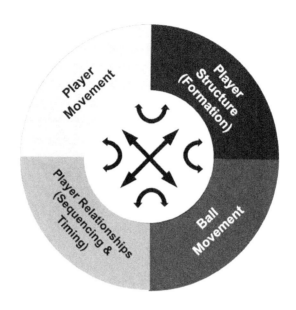

4.2.3.1   Structure and Formation

There's a reason coaches are so adamant about players aligning properly. In most football playbooks, players are expected to abide by the acronym of AAT – alignment, assignment, and technique.

Alignment comes first and demands players understand how they must structure themselves based on the play being called. Assignment dictates what players are expected to do once the ball is snapped. Finally, technique determines the movement solution for achieving that assignment. While lining up is always the first step to structure and formation, players must also understand how to position themselves once the ball is snapped. To put it succinctly, alignment is the pre-snap positioning and assignment is the post-snap positioning.

4.2.3.1.1 Lining Up

In football, properly lining up is the essence of starting effective game play. The way players line up will dictate the spacing between their teammates, how the opposing team will react to their set up, and areas into which the ball can move. Offensively, the formation is used to create opportunities for driving the field and scoring touchdowns. Defensively, it is used to prevent any form of penetration by the opposing offense and to constrain space.

4.2.3.1.2 Manipulating Field Space

No matter the offensive scheme, formation is paramount to ensuring a platform for effective play execution, even before the ball is snapped. If a team utilizes a spread option offense, a fundamental aim is to spread the defense out and create as much space as possible, forcing the opponent to cover the entire field. The offense uses formations to manipulate the field space and put the opposing defense in match-up disadvantages.

Defensively, the formation seeks to constrain the offense and prevent it from going where it wants. As a common example, coaches might tell defensive backs to line up on the inside hip of a wide receiver while in man coverage to prevent the receiver from easily going towards the middle of the field. The middle of the field allows for a much easier throw by the quarterback, whereas a long-developing throw to the outside of the field results in the ball spending more time in the air, giving defensive players more time to play the ball.

4.2.3.1.3   Field Awareness

Players that develop a knack for understanding field space by analyzing formations before and after the snap of the ball have the best understanding of where they are in relation to their teammates, their opponents, and the boundaries of the field.

This sets up big-play potential on offense because blockers can understand where the ball barrier is and where the defensive players are, allowing them to maneuver themselves into positions that set up lanes towards the end zone. On defense, field awareness can help players like deep safeties understand how quickly they need to come up and try to tackle the ball carrier in the run game without giving up space by taking a poor angle.

4.2.3.2   Ball Movement

Whether on offense or defense, when the ball moves to a certain location or even appears to move, all players will move with the ball. This falls in line with how ball speed, not player speed, dictates movement.

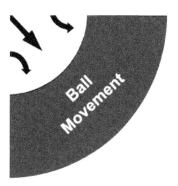

4.2.3.2.1   Putting the Ball into Space

In man coverage schemes, defensive players put their eyes on their man and go wherever he goes. In zone coverage schemes, all eyes are swiveling back to the quarterback and looking for where the ball ends up. Offenses must understand the best opportunities for ball placement against both zone defenses and man defenses. Against zone, a coach might tell a receiver to "find grass" or look for any open space in the defense's formation. Against man coverage, a receiver might be expected to run his man off vertically so that the quarterback can throw to an open receiver in the space underneath.

4.2.3.3   Player Movement

Players inevitably follow the ball. But before this, player movement is dictated by tactical assignments to help ensure all eleven players are structured properly to carry out the appropriate principles in the right moments. If players move near or away from the ball too quickly, they can risk blowing their assignments and giving the opponent an opportunity to make something happen.

4.2.3.3.1   Create or Constrain Space

On offense, player movement is dictated by a constant search for open space. If space does not exist in one area of the field, it must exist in another. The best ball carriers can perceive the full field, searching for space, and eventually reach the end zone. Alternatively, defensive player movement is based upon trying to prevent any opportunities for the offense to create space, making an impression that certain areas are off limits.

4.2.3.3.2   Misdirection & Disguise

Offensive and defensive players often use movement before or after the snap, disguising their true intentions and confusing the opponent. Quarterbacks exemplify this when they "look off" a safety in deep coverage to lure him away from the true intention of the throw.

A defense might line up as though a blitz is coming, only to back off and drop into zone coverage. If executed properly, the quarterback might assume man coverage with a blitz and preemptively decide where to throw the ball. After the snap, the assumed blitzing player drops into his zone and intercepts the ball. This type of player movement certainly ties into understanding formations and the intentions of the opponent.

4.2.3.4   Player Relationships – Sequencing and Timing

The sequence with which players move and the timing of their actions is a big-time determinant of successful play. When coaches draw up plays on a white board, they can be compared to a composer writing music. For a music composer, there is rhythm, sequencing, and timing of notes if the musical score is to sound melodious. Likewise, proper execution on the football field will reflect the rhythm, sequencing, and timing of how a team organizes the structure of the play.

Sequencing and timing are strongly based on fostering close player relationships. There's a reason why married couples in healthy relationships seem to finish each other's sentences and know each other's thoughts. A healthy team will have healthy relationships.

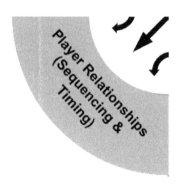

"You cannot just fool defenses with tempo. There is a difference in a fast playing team playing crisp and a fast playing team playing sloppy."

-John Schlarman

4.2.3.4.1   Communication

Football is unique because the players are not in constant motion like they are in most team sports. Instead, they line up and communicate before the ball is snapped. Communication also occurs after the snap of the ball but the most imperative verbal communication between teammates is during the lining-up process. While there might be one primary communicator (i.e. quarterback on offense or middle linebacker on defense), all players must be aware of the situation and be ready to alert the rest of the team to potential mismatches and/or big play opportunities.

In truth, most communication between players is non-verbal. Coaches can help develop this form of communication by having players practice at game-like intensities and provide them with opportunities to make decisions for themselves. Over time it can be expected to see players develop an intuitive understanding of teammate habits and instincts.

Purposely putting players in positions to diagnose situations, stay alert, and play smart - without a coach having to figuratively hold their hands throughout the learning process - provides a team with the best chance of fostering highly intelligent players who do not need to lean on the coaching staff as a crutch. Coaches then become facilitators rather than dictators, composers of the orchestra, knowing they can only guide the musicians, not play the instruments themselves.

This mindset was a philosophical point that proved critical for Pete Carroll in designing practices prior to the Seattle Seahawks' victory in Super Bowl XLVIII over the Denver Broncos. Carroll put an emphasis on abiding by principles and allowing his players to set their talents free and take ownership in pursuing their potential, rather than being pigeon-holed into a cookie-cutter performance mentality.

*"The foundation of performance is trust and confidence,
which allows you to focus."*

– Pete Carroll

4.2.3.4.2   Sequencing Action

Players must not only understand how to line up, but also where their teammates are going to be and what to do in response to the opponent after the snap of the ball. For example, a coach might give the wide receivers an "option" route, where they are expected to run one route if they see zone coverage and a completely different route if they see man coverage.

These timing, sequencing and relational components are critical, and can only come from exposure to situations that represent the game itself.

"They go really fast and try to wear the defense down or force [a] communication issue on defense so ... even if you're aligned right, if you're not able to get your assignments done quickly [and if] there's space in there, somebody gets free. The speed that they go at, it's hard to get much communication in. It forces you to kind of simplify things defensively." [vi]

-Bill Belichick on Chip Kelly's San Francisco 49ers Offense

4.2.3.4.3   Effectiveness, Efficiency and Effort

Effectiveness is the goal, and efficiency is just as important as effort. The more efficient players are, the greater their reserve of available energy, especially late in a game. This is seen when great players make skills look easy; they use as much energy as necessary, not as much as possible. However, no matter how efficiently they move, it's all for naught if effective plays aren't being made. Therefore, players must learn to become effective first, then focus on improving efficiency.

"In today's game, you might go 11, 12, or 13 plays on one drive to score. For us to run 18 plays and score 35? It didn't hit me until many years later how special that really was."

- Redskins Quarterback Doug Williams on his team's victory in Super Bowl XXIII

Tom Brady is one of seven active quarterbacks who has been sacked on less than five percent of his drop-backs over his career. This likely reflects his ability to get the ball out quickly and the skill of the Patriots' offensive line, but it's also fueled by the fact that a competitive Brady is a fast one. The burst he finds in practice often appears in games and Brady's ability to run when he needs to often confounds defenders.

"He does a great job of evading pressure – he's got a real good sense of what's going on in the pocket and no one in the game can sense it better. It may not seem like it, but he moves really, really well."[vi]

-Defensive Lineman William Hayes on Quarterback Tom Brady

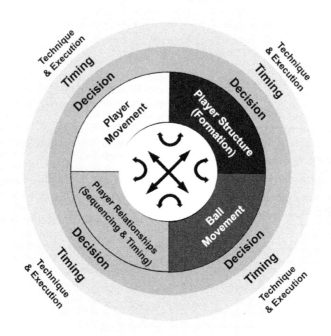

4.3 Micro-Moments

Within each Game Moment there are three distinct **Micro Moments** that help further the understanding of what is happening in the game. These Micro Moments also help identify limiting factors of team performance and can serve as a guide for shaping training and practice environments.

4.3.1 Why Micro-Moments?

The advantage of using Micro Moments is the identification of the exact time point of an event so it can be comprehended, quantified, qualified and replicated in the same context in practice in order to improve upon it before the next game.

High-level players can only improve their skill in the context in which it is executed. While a player might be able to improve on a movement-oriented concept through an isolated, closed drill, there is no optimal improvement to a player's performance in the game without exposing him to game-like scenarios that feature aspects like lining up, communicating, reading, and reacting. We isolate the Micro Moment to emphasize it in practice scenarios, *not* to practice a closed skill in isolation.

A common example is a receiver who will drop passes in practice while trying to make a catch in traffic. The receiver seems to struggle to hold onto the ball when he knows he will contact one or more defenders. Some coaches might assume it is just a catching problem, and the receiver should be sent to a JUGS machine to perform a predetermined number of catches every day after practice.

The problem with this approach is that the context is extremely limited as it relates to catching a ball from a quarterback...in traffic...while wearing pads and a helmet. Instead, a coach would be doing the player more justice by setting up a drill or situation where he must catch a ball thrown by a quarterback in the midst of pressure from a group of defenders. This way the coach can be certain that the context of the solution matches the context of the problem.

Using Micro Moments also allows for specific and intelligent use of sports science to interpret the data in context. Rather than trying to improve team performance by using global metrics like total distance covered, speed zones and high speed running, which tell us the physical demands of the game but nothing about how to win, a sports science staff can use specific Micro Moments with objectives that give the data value.

Micro Moments are primarily used by coaches, but experienced players can also benefit once they understand the basis for them. Educating players in this way helps them understand how to operate efficiently and effectively in each moment. Conveniently, the Micro Moments always occur in a linear, sequential order, making them far easier for players to understand.

For example, offensive players must always construct themselves into a formation before the ball is snapped and then penetrate the opponent's space before they successfully execute a play.

It's important to remember that no team ever operates with 100 percent efficiency, so if coaches are fully honest in their assessments, they will always find something to improve in each Micro Moment. When they discover something that needs improvement, they can work backward to distinguish how to alleviate the issues.

4.3.2   Offensive Play Micro Moments

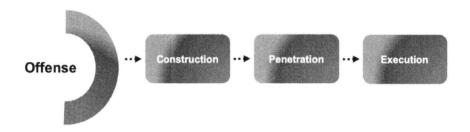

4.3.2.1   Construction – Create Usable Space

If players don't line up properly, a team is already at a disadvantage because spacing will be compromised. To construct an effective play, the formation must be taken very seriously. Spacing, motions, and the first few steps after the snap of the ball are all part of this foundation and must be organized and consistent for a successful offensive drive.

When commentators refer to an offensive coordinator "putting a solid drive together," this would also fall under the category of construction. It is not necessarily one play after another, but also the shape and movement taken on by the whole drive and how consistently the players align themselves for each play.

4.3.2.2   Penetration – Move into Opponent's Territory

Penetration follows construction and is dependent upon the formation and first movements after the snap. Successful penetration is characterized by setting up the play for a high chance of success.

Coaches might give quarterbacks read progressions in the passing game and each receiver in that progression is expected to hit the appropriate landmark. In the run game, to gain positive yards the offense needs the linemen to penetrate and move defensive players out of the way with force.

Without effective penetration, successful play execution becomes extremely hard, if not impossible.

4.3.2.3   Execution – Successfully Complete the Play

Execution comes down to finding ways to complete the play as it's designed. If players construct themselves appropriately and achieve effective penetration, then it's up to the quarterbacks, wide receivers, or running backs to make a play and get the offense closer or into the end zone.

The most important aspect of execution is to try and remove pressure from the moment. By setting up realistic practice situations that lead to the development of game intelligence (with players taking ownership of their skill set), coaches increase the likelihood of effective execution.

4.3.3   Defensive Play Micro Moments

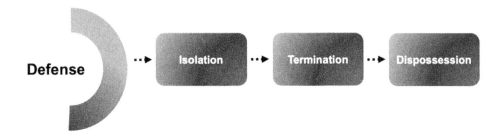

4.3.3.1   Isolation – Close Down Space

Isolation involves pursuing the ball carrier and eliminating teammates who are trying to block for him. The latter point reveals how a good defensive play might not require tackling the ball carrier at all.

The defense must act with discipline so that the defensive unit always seems to have an answer for whatever the opposing offense decides to try, so the defensive unit must also worry about its own structure and formation to stay compact and isolate ball carriers.

4.3.3.2   Termination – Remove the Play Threat

It's no mystery that offenses will almost always try and get the ball into the hands of their biggest playmakers. After isolating a ball carrier, defensive players must execute by preventing movement, tackling, or in the case of a quarterback, forcing a throw away.

If the opponent has a tremendous quarterback who can throw all day, but struggles to run the ball, then a defense's priority is on terminating the influence of the quarterback by getting pressure on him and disrupting his focus, and/or having sound coverage downfield so there are no options to which he can throw. If successful, termination will then require the opponent to rely on its less-effective run game, giving the defense the upper hand. For this reason, offenses with multiple weapons have more opportunities for mismatches and become tougher to stop, because many different players must be "terminated."

4.3.3.3   Dispossession – Regain Possession of the Ball

Ultimately, the defensive goal is to regain possession of the ball by stopping an offensive drive. In football, the simplest way of achieving this is by stopping the offense on first, second and third down and forcing it to punt away on fourth down.

Other dispossession options come in the form of turnovers (i.e. fumble recoveries, interceptions) which involve literally removing possession of the ball from the opposing offense. The teams that regularly practice dispossession often get better at turnovers.

4.3.4   Transition from Offense to Defense – Giving Up Turnovers

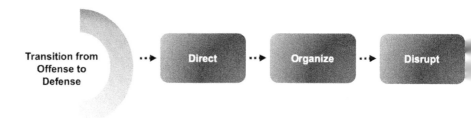

Giving up turnovers is a part of the game. While a team certainly wants to minimize the occurrence of this Game Moment, coaches and players will have to accept that at some point an interception will be thrown or fumble will be lost. Therefore, it's important to establish strategies in practice on how to mitigate the stress of this moment as much as possible.

4.3.4.1   Disrupt – Put Pressure on the Ball Carrier

As soon as a defender takes possession of the ball, it's imperative that his flow be disrupted. This takes away his initiative and forces him to slow down and think. Turnovers are extremely chaotic, so giving the ball carrier more options than he can comprehend and confusing him can help prevent a defensive touchdown.

The immediate goal is to get a body on the player and slow him down to allow for cover and support.

4.3.4.2   Organize – Stay Fortified

As the route of the player with the ball is identified, the goal is to organize and sequence players to isolate and bring him down. This requires anticipation and awareness of locating teammates and the opposing players' positions.

4.3.4.3   Direct – Send the Ball Carrier Away from the End Zone

In this moment the goal is to direct the ball carrier to run out of bounds or into the arms of pursuing teammates. At all costs, the ball carrier cannot reach the end zone. If bodies flock to the ball carrier, there is also a greater chance of forcing him to fumble the ball and the offense regaining possession.

4.3.5   Transition from Defense to Offense – Forcing Turnovers

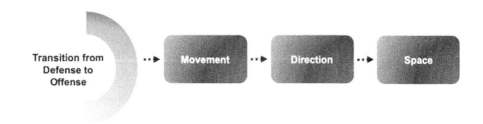

Any time the defense can force turnovers, a team has not only successfully prevented the opponent from scoring, but now has a great opportunity to put points on the board. As previously stated, turnovers are highly chaotic and hard to comprehend, so the defense must take advantage of the disorganized offense and advance the football as far as possible into opponent territory, hopefully scoring in the process.

4.3.5.1   Movement – Move the Ball Quickly
Immediately after forcing a turnover, the focus should be on movement of the ball. By moving fast, the defense gains momentum and takes initiative to get out of immediate trouble. This forces the opponent to think, slow down and react while adjusting to the change in possession. The ball carrier must be careful with the football to prevent giving it back to the opponent.

4.3.5.2   Direction – Commit to an Immediate Path
Moving the ball immediately following a turnover in a horizontal or vertical direction depends on the immediate formation of the players on the field. Teammates create the direction by identifying the best route and blocking to maximize the space in that route. It's imperative to block the player who fumbled the ball or was the intended receiver because this player is very often the one who has the best chance of tackling the defensive ball carrier.

4.3.5.3   Space – Find Room to Continue Movement
The ball carrier is now challenged with finding effective field space. Teammates must continue aiding him by finding all opportunities to make space. The fun part about when a defense forces a turnover is that there is no telling who might get the ball, so even defensive tackles must understand how to scan and stay wary of where space might be if they end up having possession of the ball.

4.4   Macro Principles
Having covered the Game Moments and their associated Micro Moments, the focus now moves to discussing the **Macro Principles** of Offensive and Defensive Play. Macro Principles are broad principles that govern proper execution in specific moments.

4.4.1   Macro Principle of Offense – Player Space

The overall objective on offense is to create space, move the ball downfield, and find opportunities to put points on the board. The offense should always be thinking about penetrating the opposing defense's space and doing whatever is necessary to get into the end zone.

When returning a kick or punt, the same Macro Principle applies. Space must be created for the ball carrier so that the ball can be advanced as far as possible in order to score. The exception is seen during punt block attempts, where returning the ball is not as much of a priority as blocking the punt and gaining better field position or scoring.

4.4.2   Macro Principle of Offense-to-Defense – Ball Pressure

After turning the ball over, the immediate action must be to pressure the new ball carrier and direct him away from the end zone. This slows the game down and allows the offensive players (who are suddenly transitioning to defense) to regain the initiative and support the teammate who is the most likely tackler. By pressuring the football, the offensive players might also have an opportunity to force a fumble and get the ball back.

4.4.3   Macro Principle of Defense – Constrain Space

The general objective on defense is to reduce opportunities for the opponent to score by pressuring players and constraining the spaces into which they can move the ball. When the word "pressure" is used, it is commonly associated with a defensive lineman putting pressure on a quarterback. But pressure can be any situation in which the offensive players are faced with conflict, whether they be ball carriers or blockers.

When kicking off or punting, the same principle applies. Players are expected to limit space and stay in their lanes of pursuit to contain the ball carrier and prevent him from gaining too many yards. The objective is to pin the kick or punt returner as far back in his own territory as possible.

The first stage of punting the ball away also encompasses aspects of offensive principles. Players first block to allow enough space for the punter to get the ball off before switching to defensive play.

4.4.4   Macro Principle of Defense-to-Offense – Ball Speed

The macro principle after forcing a turnover is to move the ball at speed. This moment features highly unstructured play, chaos and rapidly shrinking space. By moving the ball rapidly, would-be tacklers must constantly readjust and restructure. The defense that suddenly has the ball must take advantage of the opponent's disorganization by being faster than opponents can react.

4.4.5   The Importance of Macro Principles

Players who understand the Macro Principles of Offensive and Defensive Play are better able to adapt to the events of sport and handle what is in front of them.

In its simplest form, the game can be reduced to four principles: Create Space, Constrain Space, Ball Pressure, and Ball Speed. By starting with these four principles, the Game Model can be effectively structured. Remember, this is a philosophy that is taught gradually, not simply presented to the team in a power-point meeting. Successful teams are built based on an understanding of clear, global principles associated with a complex system that appears intricate when functioning efficiently and effectively.

As an example, if offensive players understand the importance of creating space, they will view every action they take to accomplish that Macro Principle. Likewise, defensive players who understand the Macro Principle of defense will know they simply cannot give up space...no matter what.

> *"I don't really say, 'Call this specific play' or 'Call this specific defense.' I might say 'We need to run the ball a little more,' 'We need to pressure the quarterback a little more,' 'Our pressures are not effective' (or) 'We need to try to cover.' It's more general and philosophical."* [viii]

> *-Nick Saban*

4.5 Micro Principles

Each Macro Principle is composed of **Micro Principles** – small, focused principles that help evolve an understanding of how to accomplish the desired goals of offensive and defensive play.

4.5.1 Micro Principles of Offensive Play

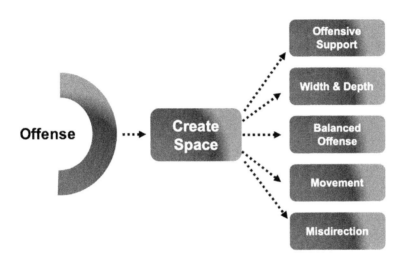

There is a lot of talk about creating space when it comes to Offensive Play, but accomplishing this goal is not always easy. Creating space is a result of smaller building blocks that come together into an effective whole. These Micro Principles provide a blueprint for developing the smaller components, so that creation of space is possible.

4.5.1.1 Offensive Support – Create Big Play Opportunities

When offensive players support each other, more space can be created through construction of different formations and motions, and the use of different ball carriers. This will give the defense too many options to defend, which will wear it down and dramatically slow its decision-making. If all offensive players are on the same page, big plays are likely to happen.

Some teams use **focused support**, such as the old-school ground-and-pound style of offense, where the challenge for the defense lies in executing effectively while anticipating the upcoming play. Most teams now utilize a **massed support**, in which the offense has multiple attacking options that make it tough for the defense to predict what is coming.

Offensive support really lies in the scheme's identity and ensuring that all players are operating on the same page.

4.5.1.2 Width and Depth – Make the Field as Big as Possible

Attacking the perimeter of the field should always exist in harmony with attacking downfield and a balanced offense requires making the field as big as possible in all directions. Attacking the perimeter becomes increasingly important as the field gets shorter and wider, such as in the red zone or during goal line situations.

Offenses spread the field using formations, motioning players before the snap, or varying player movement after the snap. In the latter case, a coach might make use of natural picking patterns where different receivers cross paths in complex ways to throw off the defenders and open room for the quarterback to throw a completion to a player in space.

For most offenses, it is important to establish perimeter threats early so the defense is forced to honor players that line up or move near the boundary, creating more space for attacking downfield when desired. Going vertically downfield (or at least having that threat) is essential because this is the area that will give ball carriers a more direct route to the end zone.

The fastest path between any two points is a straight line. So, if an offense can give the ball carrier an opportunity to run in a straight line towards the end zone, the chances of scoring become much higher. This can be achieved through a downhill run game or a passing attack that takes shots vertically to receivers running deeper routes.

4.5.1.3   Balanced Offense – Use Multiple Attacking Options

A balanced offensive system has options for attacking the perimeter, attacking downfield, and utilizing a mix of run and pass plays to accomplish both. Other options include designed fakes and trick plays.

An offense can have a definitive style (i.e. ground-and-pound, air raid, etc.), but still have other viable options in case the effectiveness of the primary strategy starts to diminish. A balanced offense allows for adaptability and makes it much harder for a defense to stop the attack.

4.5.1.4   Movement – Spread the Ball to Different Players

Not only is it important to create effective field space, but it's also crucial to put the ball in different players' hands as much as possible. Many offenses rely on a small number of big playmakers, but a truly efficient offensive attack is the result of having multiple players with big play ability.

When many players add value to an offense, opposing defenses will struggle with gaining comfort in matchups. This is where skill development in practice is important. By improving the ability of players who are lower on the depth chart, more options arise, and less panic ensues when the primary attack is stopped or when big-time players experience injuries.

"[A concept] may have been depressed in the past few years because we didn't have anybody to do it. Injury-wise, you lose a guy. Or somebody is not there very often. Whatever it may be. But the offense hasn't changed. The offense revolves around the ability of the guys who can run it." [ix]

-Ivan Fears on the Patriots' Offense

4.5.1.5   Misdirection –Hiding True Intentions

Misdirection involves using formations, motions, fakes, decoys or other trick plays to throw the defense off and hide true intentions. Often described as "window dressing," using misdirection challenges the ability of the opposing defense to stay true to keys and not let eyes wander. The more realistic an offense can make a misdirection appear, the more of a key-breaking stimulus it will become, leaving the defense far more challenged when locating the ball.

4.5.2   Micro Principles of Defensive Play

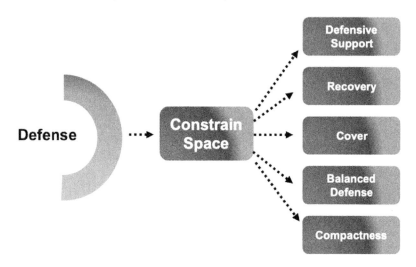

The Macro Principle for Defensive Play is to constrain space. The Micro Principles will provide more insight as to how that aim can be accomplished. Effective Defensive Play is reliant on the ability to abide by these Micro Principles in the defensive moment.

4.5.2.1   Defensive Support – Do Your Job

Defensive players must do their best to avoid selfishness and understand how their actions affect the other ten players on their side of the ball. For isolation to occur, a defense must work together to remove all chances of the ball carrier finding space. Communication becomes imperative, and all eleven players must understand their roles and the roles of their teammates to build support for each other.

4.5.2.2   Recovery – Take Back Momentum

Recovery of momentum is primarily psychological in nature. Momentum is lost after the opponent successfully completes a big play or scores. When this happens, nothing is more important than regaining the momentum on the next drive.

Defenses that are adapted to handling chaos are better able to recover momentum and return to the primary job at hand: applying pressure.

4.5.2.3 Cover – Take Up Space

Offensive players seek to find holes and gaps in the defense and take advantage of available space. Defensively, it's important to maintain balance and put players in positions to cover space. Zone coverage is a perfect example of how players will drop to different zones to cover certain spaces on the field. Conversely, man coverage will take away an offensive player's personal space, causing major discomfort as he attempts to move around the field.

If defensive players can properly cover space in both zone and man coverage, putting pressure on the ball carrier becomes much easier since there should always be at least one defender present to start isolating the ball carrier.

4.5.2.4 Balanced Defense – Hold Off Various Attacks

Just as a balanced offense requires a strong mix of plays to spread the field in all directions, a balanced defense must constrain the field and make it as small as possible. A balanced defense can prevent an offense from attacking the perimeter and can also run with any offensive player attempting to go vertically down the field. Not only does communication become important but developing the proper perceptual abilities – such as key-read progressions – will directly impact defensive players' ability to be in the right place at the right time to make a play.

4.5.2.5 Compactness – Working to Prevent Penetration

A defense that stays compact poses a major threat to offensive schemes. As a perfect metaphor for defensive compactness, the "Steel Curtain" of the Pittsburgh Steelers in the 1970s made it extremely difficult for ball carriers to make big plays. There always seemed to be a Steeler defender ready to swallow them up.

The less opportunity for an offense to make easy gains up the field, the more demoralized offensive players becomes. A compact defense forces the offense to be more meticulous. The goal is for offensive players to become more self-conscious of their actions, which can reduce their ability to get into a fluid rhythm.

4.6   Visualizing the Game Model

Let's review what we've discussed thus far:

- Every game is composed of Game Moments.
- The four moments are Offense, Defense, Transition from Offense-to-Defense, and Transition from Defense-to-Offense.
- Each Game Moment has a set of Micro Moments that always occur in sequence (i.e. construction, penetration, and execution).
- In any Game Moment, both teams deal with the over-arching Game Principles of formation, ball movement, player movement, and the relationships between the players in terms of timing/sequencing of actions. These principles are always present.
- Each Game Moment has its own set of sub-principles known as Macro Principles which will change whether amid Offensive Play, Defensive Play, or dealing with turnovers.
- The Macro Principle of Offensive Play is to create space, which is realized through offensive support, width, depth, balanced offense, movement, and misdirection.
- The Macro Principle of Defensive Play is to constrain space, which is accomplished through defensive support, recovery of momentum, covering space, defensive balance, and maintaining compactness.

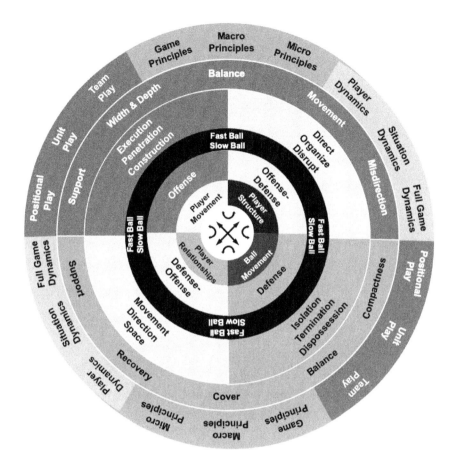

67

4.6.1   Using the Game Model to Improve Performance

All the factors discussed previously can be considered common sense for most coaches. The beauty of the Game Model lies in its simplicity of comprehension. Remember, the goal of a Game Model is for players and support staff members to easily understand what contributes to effective game play so that there is no confusion, and nothing gets forgotten.

Let's consider an example of how the Game Model can be used to qualitatively assess a team's performance and provide a window for developing solutions. Consider the following hypothetical scenario:

A defensive coordinator stresses to his players that he wants to have dominant Defensive Play. The Macro Principle of Defensive Play is to constrain space. So, all week in practice, he tells his players to get to the football as fast as they can.

The team plays their season opener against an opponent that they expect to beat easily. During the game, the defense gives up big plays in every quarter. In the end, the team loses by a pretty large margin. This wasn't the performance that the defensive coordinator was anticipating.

The defensive coordinator goes to the film room after the game and reviews what happened. Using the Game Model as a guide, he looks to the Micro Principles of Defensive Play as a checklist to assess and make comments regarding the defensive unit's performance.

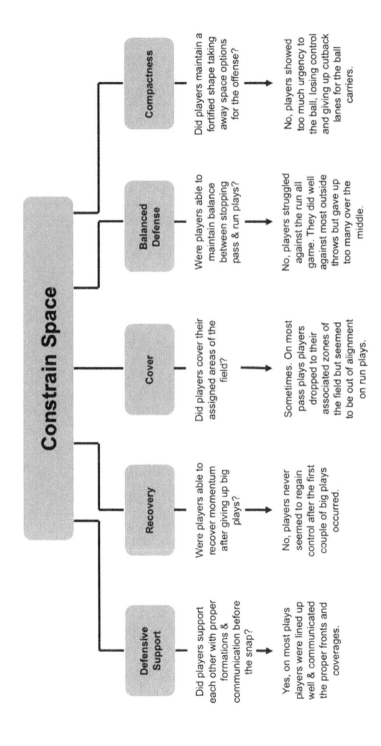

Constrain Space

Defensive Support

Did players support each other with proper formations & communication before the snap?

Yes, on most plays players were lined up well & communicated the proper fronts and coverages.

Recovery

Were players able to recover momentum after giving up big plays?

No, players never seemed to regain control after the first couple of big plays occurred.

Cover

Did players cover their assigned areas of the field?

Sometimes. On most pass plays players dropped to their associated zones of the field but seemed to be out of alignment on run plays.

Balanced Defense

Were players able to maintain balance between stopping pass & run plays?

No, players struggled against the run all game. They did well against most outside throws but gave up too many over the middle.

Compactness

Did players maintain a fortified shape taking away space options for the offense?

No, players showed too much urgency to the ball, losing control and giving up cutback lanes for the ball carriers.

From here, the defensive coordinator determines the greatest problem and wonders if solving it would help alleviate the other problems. He realizes that it was the defense's inability to maintain compactness that caused the other problems to occur.

Since the defensive coordinator had stressed all week in practice for the players to sprint full speed to the ball (remember the need for "optimal velocity" over maximum velocity), his players were actually doing more than necessary and found themselves out of position at the point of attack.

As a result, they lost their compactness, struggled to maintain a balance, and gave up the spaces they were covering. Furthermore, they became so psychologically distraught that they simply could not recover the momentum.

The defensive coordinator then takes this information and decides to solve it in upcoming practices by focusing on the importance of how to properly isolate a ball carrier. He emphasizes attacking under control and building the awareness of teammate location, so the players can send the ball towards support, rather than trying to do too much on their own to make plays.

4.7   Building Team Cohesion with Communication

Clear communication of the Game Principles, Macro Principles, and Micro Principles helps ensure that none of the consistent messages to the team are conflicting or contradictory. This helps players own the process and develop through strong teaching from the coaches. The Game Model is also important for recruiting or drafting future eligible players who can represent and execute the Game Plan accordingly.

Most players who become "busts" have more than enough skill. Often, these players underperform as a result of attitudes, emotions or other psychological issues. Therefore, the Game Model must also consider players' psychological preparation as it relates to the tactical and technical abilities that coaches want to see. Coherence helps players understand what is expected of them within the team identity. This helps us formulate the Game Plan and playbook.

If a coach wants a swarming defense that isolates and terminates the ball carrier, then he should relay this message to his defensive players as much as possible. This way, they will come to understand how to devote their energy in training and practice to achieve what is expected of them on the field. If coaches see a player who consistently decides not to swarm to the football, he will not be a player that fits the team's outlook.

The same idea can be applied to offense. If a coach expects his players to line up quickly and have great discipline in their alignments, then any player who is too lazy to line up in his designated spot will not be an asset. The players that best match the coach's interpretation of the Game Model will give the team the most production.

When players adopt and accept the Game Model, they can start to show an understanding and expectation of their teammates' actions before they even happen. This is where coherence at the team level can come to life and a team will appear to operate as a functional whole, rather than just a collection of individual players. The whole is greater than the sum of its parts.

Cohesion and coherence are dependent on communication. This goes beyond the coaching staff and players. Anyone who will have direct contact with the players must be on the same page. A clear, consistent message should flow among all levels of the organization in an unconscious, subliminal manner. This is where having consistent language is important so that the entire organization understands, evaluates and adapts in an aligned manner.

4.7.1   Developing Organizational Focus

When players understand the Game Model, they will personify the organization's focus. This means that the aims of the team identity will be so engrained in the players that the coaches can feel comfortable allowing the players to take the initiative in chaotic situations, rather than micro-managing them. Organizational focus can help connect players and player groups, so they work concurrently at several levels.

"My philosophy, really, is that less is more, so I'd rather have fewer people doing more work than more people doing a little more work. As long as everybody is busy, as long as everybody feels productive, they feel good about what they're doing and they feel like they're contributing; I think when people have lag time and kind of not enough to do, that leads to getting distracted and complaining or being less productive. So even though you have more people, sometimes less work gets done."

- Bill Belichick

4.7.2 Avoiding Conflicting Interests

Swaying from consistent terminology can only have a negative impact on a team. For instance, if the defensive line coach preaches a technique to the defensive line, but then the head coach turns around and says something totally different, the players will get confused and the intent of the playbook becomes muddled. If players are not sure what they are expected to do, then they cannot be expected to operate effectively during the game.

Another potential conflict is if the strength and conditioning coaches, or sports science staff, become over-reliant on performance numbers that may or may not have much influence over how players prepare for games. These are arguably the most crucial support staff members, since they spend a great deal of time with players and directly impact their physical readiness for practice and games.

If the strength coaches and/or sports science staff obsess over certain data points, they may start to distract the players with activities that are not coherent with what is happening in practice, perhaps taking away from acquiring greater skill and tactical awareness.

The most important forms of preparation for any player are skill acquisition and tactical knowledge, both of which are developed by practicing and playing the sport. So, the primary job of the strength and conditioning and sports science personnel is to ensure that players are fit and healthy enough to stay on the field.

4.7.3   Finding Solutions, Not Dwelling on Errors

When assessing team performance, it's important to always try and find solutions rather than spending more time than necessary having emotional reactions to what went wrong in the last game. The Game Model can help with this.

When watching film, coaches can first look for structure and formation. Are the players positioned properly? Then they can move toward looking at aspects of player movement, ball movement, and player relationships. The Game Model is a road map to understanding the game in context, giving coaches the opportunity to find solutions in context.

The overall objective for any team is obvious - win the game. In comparison to winning, all other aims are secondary and must be cohesive with finding ways to win. The Game Model ensures coaches can help players understand how to operate from a series of principles. When players thoroughly understand the Game Model principles, all specific components of a Game Plan or playbook will be learned and retained at a faster rate.

If players, coaches, and support staff do not understand the principles that are in place to generate wins, then the team will fail to create a plan leading to the big picture imperative. At all costs, having anyone in the organization chasing selfish goals that subvert or even sabotage the overall intention to win must be avoided. In order to keep an organization intact, the team must win games. Communication helps everyone get there.

5 Preparing the Player

In sport, the next game is the only one that matters. Great coaches understand that every available minute of preparation must be used maximally and purposefully. The Game Model provides a foundational blueprint to help accurately assess performance in practice and games. With it, coaches become knowledgeable about how to find solutions and improve.

Structuring the week is also very important. While the theory behind the Game Model sounds simplistic, when it comes to how players perform coaches are dealing with complex human beings. Trying to get them to behave in a desirable manner is an intricate challenge, one that requires some knowledge as to how humans operate, not the least of which includes how they handle stress and recover from it.

Yes, it's important to maximize every moment of preparation, but one must also respect players as *people first*. People deal with the stresses of life, only adding to what they experience in a weight room or on a football field. It is a staff's responsibility to get a better understanding of stress and how to manage it appropriately so that performance is maximized on game day.

5.1 People are Creatures of Habit

Despite an instinct for control, a coach's role is not to micromanage. Rather, coaches must help instill positive and sustainable habits, so players find their own avenues to success and continually learn, grow, and develop. To put it concisely, coaches are *performance facilitators*.

Humans seem to function more efficiently when their bodies experience a repeated cycle, allowing their "biological clock" (also known as circadian rhythm) to recognize consistent patterns. Such consistency means their bodies can adapt and learn to be more resourceful and recover faster when it comes to dealing with stress.[xi]

It is also necessary to consider that people exist within societal cycles. Therefore, one might see changes in player behaviors from season to season or between starting the winter off-season versus starting training camp in the summer. While these can (and are) often ignored by many, they are often the basis of stable lifestyles and of paramount importance to relationships between coaches and players, players and players, and players and families.

5.1.1   The Need for Consistent Routines

In order to construct a sustainable, winning program, coaches must respect the influence of society on players and, just as importantly, on their friends, family and loved ones. These are the people around them 24/7 and comprise a players' personal environmental bubble.

For example, in most situations professional players are a major influence on the family schedule. If the pattern or schedule to which they adhere is inconsistent or in direct conflict with the cycles and patterns of everyone else in the family, it can cause conflict. Respecting the importance of home life and family cannot be undervalued.

When family members know that the team has the same day off each week, they can plan around it, especially for events like children's birthday parties or family visits. Irregular weekly patterns disrupt family plans and schedules. Players are people and should not be expected to dismiss their outside support network.

Respecting the importance of home life and family
cannot be undervalued.

Players do not exist only as part of a sports team; they're also part of social groups away from team facilities. Coaches must consider player needs within the context of these groups. In retrospect, the length of a career in sport is incredibly short in comparison to a lifetime. If players only identify as athletes, they risk experiencing dysfunction when their sport careers are over. People first, players second.

For these reasons, the weekly approach that we present later provides a clear plan for what will happen on each day. With this construct, a player knows that he can schedule free time with his spouse, significant other, kids, parents, or friends on scheduled off days. Having consistent and repeatable habits is crucial for a healthy environment outside of sport.

This routine will also benefit the coaching staff. Like players, coaches are people with friends and families. Providing a predictable, consistent structure for players, coaches and staff members allows everyone to live their lives more easily and with less friction and worry.

As a bonus, once a team has established a familiar system and routine, the weekly training stimuli will be less stressful to the players, since they have already adapted to the weekly routine. This will leave them fresher for practices and games. To achieve consistency, an organization must have a set of routines for every scenario, such as preparing for a Thursday night football game after having just played on Sunday, facing back-to-back away games, or having several more weeks to get ready for the college football playoffs. The game is already chaotic enough as it is - implementing inconsistent, random weekly routines will only lead to unmanageability.

As another example, if players come to learn that every Wednesday during the season will include a high-intensity, high-collision Olympic weightlifting session, their bodies come to anticipate this stimulus. Afterward, if the nutrition and therapy staffs have encouraged the players to consume a high-protein meal and take part in restorative activities, the appropriate body systems are primed for recovery and growth by the familiar pattern. Optimizing such patterns means that players will have deeper energy reserves on which to draw come game day.

"I've gotta continue to do a better job of figuring out that work-life balance. Being able to shut off. Because...you're kinda always just thinking through things. Your mind's always racing. And I– I know that it can't be healthy to continue to do this for a long time. But while– while you're able to do it and feel like you've got some energy, you sure love it."[xix]

-Sean McVay

5.1.2   Communication and Team Dynamics

A player's societal environment can certainly impact him in a negative way. Players can easily and often associate with "the wrong crowd" and find themselves in situations leading to poor decisions. This is a major reason why communication is such an important component of the Game Model.

If coaches and scouts only focus on a player's skill set and physical ability (rather than getting to know him as a human being), then they will be unable to foresee any societal influences that might affect that player's psychological health. By showing players that they genuinely care about them, coaches will make players feel like they belong to something sincere.

Treating all players this way can help foster positive team dynamics throughout the building. Team culture is paramount, and communication is at the center of it all.

5.1.3   The Big Picture of Stress

Developing positive habits in players is about more than making sure they can play at a high level on game day. It is also a team's responsibility to ensure that players are kept healthy and their stress loads managed as best as possible. Many become misguided into thinking that if players are moving fast or feeling strong then they are fully healthy. The next section explores the big picture of keeping a player healthy and functioning at a high level.

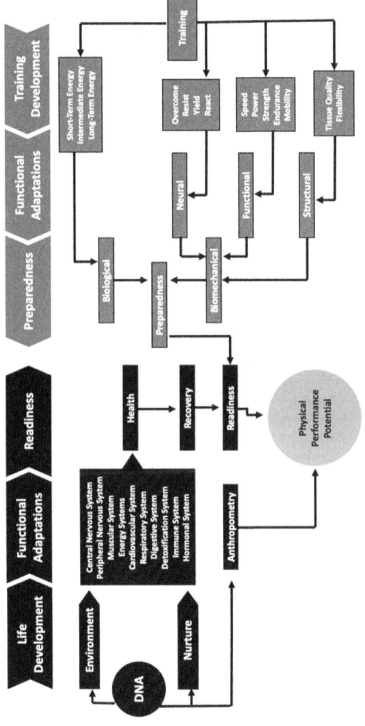

79

5.2   The Four-Coactive Model of Player Preparation

Contrary to common belief, the physical make-up of a player (considered in isolation) does *not* determine his success on the field. Anyone who follows football closely will be able to tell you that most first-round NFL draft picks are selected primarily due to their physical abilities. Once selected, commentators often boast about how the player had amazing numbers at the NFL Combine, how tall the player is, what his wingspan might be, how big his hands are, and other noteworthy metrics.

The irony is that if one considers the players who consistently make it to the Pro Bowl and eventually into the Hall of Fame, the list of names often includes several players who were *not* considered physical specimens. Names like Jerry Rice come to mind. Although Rice was selected in the first round of the 1985 NFL Draft by the San Francisco 49ers, he was criticized for being "slow" because he ran a 40-yard dash time of 4.71 seconds.

Kurt Warner is another example, having gone through several seasons of playing arena football and NFL Europe before signing a contract with the St. Louis Rams in 1998. He saw limited action in his first season, then took advantage of an opportunity in 1999 when starting quarterback Trent Green went down with an injury. Warner went on to lead the "greatest show on turf," becoming a winner and MVP of Super Bowl XXXIV.[xii]

In today's NFL, perhaps no example is greater than Tom Brady of the New England Patriots. Brady was evaluated as a very low prospect before being selected in the sixth round of the 2000 NFL Draft by New England. Since then, he has gone out and become arguably the greatest quarterback to ever play the game, with six Super Bowl championships to show for it. How did all those other teams miss Brady's potential? Maybe they were only looking at Brady's physical make-up, which was not considered impressive.

Physical prowess is only one factor in terms of what goes into being a successful player. We cannot isolate the physical ability of a player without considering how it interacts with his psychological well-being, his technical skill, and his tactical awareness and knowledge of the game.

Based on these aspects, we present a Four-Coactive Model. In it, there are four elements of player preparation, all of which are intertwined and interdependent:

1. Tactical Preparation
2. Technical Preparation
3. Psychological Preparation
4. Physical Preparation

All four elements are present to varying degrees in every moment of the game. They are also present during all forms of practice and preparation. They are called "coactives" because they both complement and rely upon each other. These four coactives must come together in a synchronized manner for the player to execute effectively. They cannot exist without each other. They are complementary, codependent, and co-reliant.

Without good health, no other form of preparation will matter in the long run.

It is a mistake to think about these four coactives without considering the most vital aspect of player preparation: health. Player health is an essential umbrella that affects all four coactives. Without health, none of the other coactives matter in the long run.

5.3   The Tactical Coactive

When it comes to game-day performance, each player's tactical acumen is the front-runner of the four coactives. If players don't understand what to do when they're on the field, then they simply can't help a team win. When assessing performance, coaches often attribute failures of execution to physical shortcomings. But often, high-level players have more than enough physical competence to do what is needed. After all, they are recruited for this purpose.

Instead, what we typically find is that unsuccessful players lack the requisite tactical know-how. This also means that just because a player is a physical specimen, he is not excused from understanding how to position himself on the field or adhering to the play calls.

One element of tactical preparation that's often overlooked is improving player decision-making on the field. The exercises, drills, and games designed for training and practice should focus on the desired tactical outcome at the individual, unit, and team level. This will help players perform by focusing on successfully completing the task rather than being overly self-conscious of their movement.

Learning opportunities are dictated by what the current scenario looks like and what players can draw on from their past experiences. This is exactly how they will operate in the game. It's essential that tactical team periods of practice and scrimmages occur at (or above) game tempo so that the players learn to execute under pressure on game day.

When assessing performance, we should not attribute
failures of execution to physical shortcomings alone.

The tactical preparation is based on the next game on the calendar. While maintaining team principles, coaches might recognize a dominant quality in the opposing team that needs to be mitigated, such as the threat of a game-breaking player who can score on any given play. Coaches might also find a limiting factor in the opposing team that can be exploited, so they can design tactics to take advantage of this.

Developing tactical awareness is more inclusive than just running through plays on the field. This form of training is highly cognitive in nature. Film study, white board work, walk-throughs and situational awareness are all forms of tactical preparation.

Just like the other coactives, the tactical coactive creates a stress load on players, but this stress affects their brains more than on their bodies. While film study might not be physically stressing for players, the duration must be considered as part of the cumulative stress load for the day.

Coaches simply cannot put players through high-intensity, high-volume sessions across all four coactives, day after day. If they do, they'll compromise learning outcomes, and the players will be worn down going into the next game. Therefore, the tactical sessions must be balanced with all other stressors during the weekly cycle of training.

5.3.1   Tactical Context and Moments

As with everything else, player tactical skills need to be developed within the framework of the Game Model. If a player understands his role in the film room but can't seem to apply it on the field or during the game, then it's useless.

When trying to improve players' tactical capabilities, coaches can look at the Micro Moments. While several things may need attention, it is most efficient to pick just one focal point per moment in the upcoming practice week. As an example, if the wide receivers line up correctly but tend to run improper routes, then coaches will know they are not struggling in the moment of construction but need to focus on the moment of penetration.

By using this targeted approach, coaches can create informed drills to use in the week's practices. They will know exactly which player (or players) are expected to execute in the relevant Micro Moments. For example, a defensive back may develop great skill in covering various opponents in man coverage, but he must still know who to cover on each play. This is where tactical awareness affects/meets technical skill.

5.3.2   The Tactical To-Do List

Coaches can look to the Game Model and the Macro Principles to formulate a tactical to-do list. For example, drills and team periods will always focus on the Game Principles of ball movement, player movement, formations/positioning, and the relationships between players. The side of the ball that adheres best to the Game Principles will be the side that wins. So, coaches must always consider how they want the team to operate amongst these principles.

> *"We made some changes during the year. We always make changes. It's a process you go through. You put players in certain situations and certain groupings together...some work better than others...maybe you see more potential in a certain player or group of players...and you decide to move forward more with that or maybe you do it less because you don't feel as good about it...it's just an ongoing process. It doesn't happen overnight."* [xiv]

> *- Bill Belichick*

For example, an offensive coordinator may want to use a spread offense with a high tempo to execute fast ball movement. He can design drills and situations that require the quarterbacks to get the ball to a variety of receivers in the passing game.

He can use the scout team to take away certain players so the quarterback can't consecutively throw to a favorite target.

Within the same system, the running backs coach might focus on the movement of his players to ensure that they can help the quarterback have a legitimate passing option by checking the ball down to them. During pass skeleton or seven-on-seven situations, all the receivers (running backs included) can work on their sequencing in relation to each other and on recognizing the actions of their opponents on the defensive side to help the quarterback find an effective passing target.

The Macro and Micro Principles will help further break down the players' execution and can be used to design drills to achieve tactical goals. While Offensive Play will achieve the Game Principles by creating space, Defensive Play will do so by constraining space and putting pressure on the ball carriers. Every offensive and defensive drill should emphasize the Macro Principles: create space for Offensive Play, constrain space for Defensive Play.

> *The Macro and Micro Principles will help us further break down the players' execution and design drills to achieve tactical goals*

5.3.3   Game Model Drill Design

By designing practice drills based upon the moments and principles of the Game Model, coaches will have a direct blueprint of how to assess each player and determine where the limiting factors of performance might exist.

If a linebacker hesitates too much in the run game and allows the opposing linemen to block him, creating space for the running back, then that is a limiting factor that directly goes against the principles of Defensive Play. Thus, the linebacker coach can design drills to help the player learn how to observe and act faster and improve his technical ability within a tactical framework.

5.4   The Technical Coactive

A player's technical skill is an oft-misunderstood form of preparation. In the same way that scouts and commentators over-emphasize a player's physical make-up, they also over-emphasize a player's movement, attempting to fit it into a perfect, one-size-fits-all technical model.

However, recent theories on motor control like dynamical systems theory and ecological dynamics suggest the futility of this approach, namely that it is impossible for a player to move exactly the same way twice.[iv] Even if he could, it wouldn't be warranted because the opponents, situations, environments, and other contextual elements of the game are constantly changing.

Therefore, the goal is to build players who move in dynamic, adaptable, and resilient ways to accomplish tactical goals.

5.4.1   Spatial Awareness

The first step in coaching technical skill is to teach players to understand their position and how it relates to those around them. In this way, players will comprehend how to manipulate the space available to them. This is **spatial awareness,** and it depends on the ability to process what is happening on the field and how the environment will change.

When a player is described as having great "vision," it is really his perception and ability to process visual information which ultimately dictates the type of physical action he chooses. Contrary to popular belief, vision, perception, and game-specific spatial awareness *can* be developed and trained by engaging in learning tasks that represent aspects of the game.

When football players are prepared using representative learning in practice, they will be able to focus more during the unexpected events that occur in the game and feel less overwhelmed. Players will be less self-conscious of their movements and will be paying more attention to what is happening around them, acting through instinct.

Over the past half century, American fighter pilot John Boyd was one of the greatest thinkers on the topic of relating observation and action. Boyd developed theories as to how American fighter jets were victorious over Russian MiGs even though the Russians had comparable (and in some ways better) technology. He deduced that the cockpits in American planes afforded pilots greater visibility, which enabled them to orient themselves quicker than their Russian adversaries and perform desired actions faster.[xvi]

There is a connection between Boyd's theories and performance in sport. Success does not really come down to having faster, more physical players...it comes down to having players who make faster, more effective decisions. This falls in line with Boyd's OODA Loop, also known as the "observation-action cycle," which consists of four stages:

1. **Observe**: Employ our senses to detect what is going on around us and apply our situational awareness to inform our assessment.
2. **Orient**: Focus our attention on what we've just observed and decide what it means in context. Here, we make assumptions, judgments, and evaluations based on the available information.
3. **Decide**: Using a combination of what we're currently experiencing and our prior experiences, we select a movement pattern to achieve our desired aim. This decision can be self-contained, such as a player deciding to move with the ball, or it might involve teammates.
4. **Act**: Keeping our game plan aims in mind, we put our decision into action. As soon as this stage of the cycle ends, the first phase begins again.

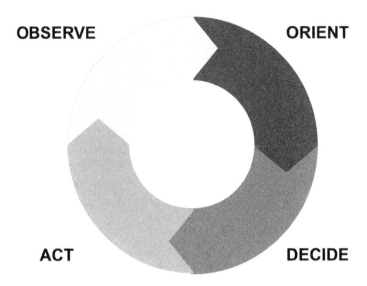

OBSERVE   **ORIENT**

ACT   **DECIDE**

An interesting note on the OODA loop is how the orientation stage depends on a host of factors, as seen in the figure on the next page. While not typically considered, cultural traditions and genetic heritage can impact how people perceive information and cultures help formulate a person's idea of the world from the time he/she is born.

Anything that plays a part in shaping behavior will have an effect during the orientation stage and will influence the decisions a person makes. Even in the most thoughtfully designed practice situations, the truth is that predicting a person's behavior is incredibly complex.

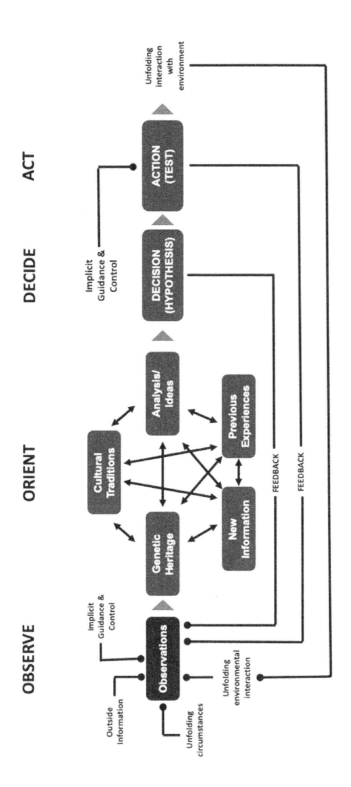

5.4.3   The Importance of Context

Context is king. To make preparation more optimal, coaches must constantly keep the context of the game in mind. One should never look at the execution of a skill without considering the context.

Just because a player has great "footwork" when he works out by himself on an agility ladder does not mean he will be able to function well within the context of the game. When receivers and defensive backs perform positional movement skills in isolation - like running routes on air or performing a series of backpedal patterns - they will only have to account for their own body moving in space. This might be fine for a warmup routine, but it will do very little for transfer to the game.

Transfer to game performance requires perceptual triggers against which to observe and act. These must also be considered in context. For example, adding non-specific perceptual triggers like a coach pointing in a certain direction can help build general reactive ability, but will still lie far outside the game context. It's not enough to have players reacting to *something*, the experience must be game-like in order to improve sport performance.

If a receiver and defensive back were to instead perform one-on-ones against each other, they would then add more game-like context to their training. Thus, the players would be more concerned with accomplishing a specific sport task rather than being self-conscious about their own movement. Their skill development would now be more organic because the observations would dictate the actions, rather than the actions simply being performed for the sake of moving.

Context is King

Contextualized activities can be layered in terms of complexity. By adding more players and running a seven-on-seven practice, the players must not only account for their opponents, but also their relationship to teammates, making the overall complexity higher than one-on-one situations. Progressing to eleven-on-eleven team periods will produce an environment that is very similar to the game itself. These layers indicate rising complexity where perception of the environment will take on an increasing role.

Even when players look like they're exhibiting consistent form in skill execution during a game, they are making slightly different movements each time. The best players are those who can operate along a movement bandwidth in which a similar skill can be performed against a variety of constraints and environments. This means that the outputs are consistent in terms of *results* – like a player beating the man across from him repeatedly – but the *manifestation* of the result happens in different ways.

Great players are capable of consistently completing tasks by adapting movement solutions to fit the problems they face – all without losing efficiency of movement or effectiveness of solutions. Technical mastery has less to do with how a player moves in a "closed" environment – in the absence of opponents – and more to do with how that player is able to solve varying sport problems with efficient and effective movement solutions.

Field position, proximity to the end zone, opponents, teammates, ball speed, play call, formation, and time on the play clock are just a few of the many constraints that require players to change how they perform any skill in various Game Moments. Additionally, environmental factors - bad weather, crowd noise, and the condition of the playing surface – also shape such moments. Therefore, in a game setting, a skill is never performed the same way twice.

The bottom line is that we cannot learn a skill in isolation and expect it to fully translate to a game setting.

5.4.4   The Lock and the Key

Effective technical ability is about choosing the right skill in any given situation. This is basically about selecting the right tool from the toolbox. Correct pattern recall is the precursor to effective action. It can't be said that a quarterback made a "good pass" or a "bad pass" unless one looks at the context in which the throw was made.

For example, one can argue that a wobbly, ugly throw is "bad" compared to a straight, spiraling throw. But if the ugly throw goes for a touchdown, it's the right pass. Likewise, a deep throw with a perfect spiral that gets intercepted is the wrong pass. It's all about context.

Perhaps a better analogy is one of a lock and key. The right key is needed to open a specific door, just as the right movement is needed to accomplish a specific sport task. The right "key" will be dependent on the individual player and the available toolbox he has at his disposal from accrued time of practice and learning.

Consider a pass rusher working his moves against a stationary tackle bag. He might work his spin move, his dip and rip, his chop and swipe, or whatever he wants. In this situation, the player has a bunch of "keys" available to him, but he will never know which keys open the right doors. What if he goes for a spin move and the offensive lineman is there waiting for him, pancaking him while his back is turned?

Learning the moves in isolation won't help him get to the quarterback. He must understand the context and discover which keys will open which doors when the right opportunities present themselves. Decision-making is not a stop-and-start system but involves a constant feedback loop.

5.4.5   Technical Execution

It's not enough to know what to do in a football game; players must also do it quickly enough and with the right amount of power, precision and direction to be effective. Therefore, it's imperative that coaches allow players to practice at different levels of complexity based on the game. When given the proper perceptual environment, player skill development and retention will be long-term.

Using the pass rusher example from before, spending practice time having him work against a tackle bag rather than against an actual opponent will lead to difficulty for him in understanding when and why to use certain skills. This means that when it's game time, his execution will be slower because he has had less exposure to realistic scenarios.

The same concept applies to a defensive back who is expected to shut down a receiver in man coverage. Having him perform backpedal drills until the cows come home won't help him much. He needs to see a variety of different receivers and learn to perceive their actions and find the right "key" for the "lock" – the right movement skill for the sport problem.

5.4.6   Technical and Tactical Synergy

For players to perform effectively and achieve the objectives of the Game Plan, sufficient technical skill or tactical awareness in isolation are not enough – players must have both. A quarterback might be able to execute a beautiful throw, but if he doesn't have the tactical know-how to predict where a teammate will be then his passing skills will not help his team win. Similarly, if a running back knows where he needs to position himself during a play but lacks the technique needed to perform his task, the offense will fail to score or will lose possession. Technical and tactical synergy is crucial.

5.5   The Psychological Coactive

When profiling or assessing a player from a psychological perspective, there are three micro coactives: spirituality, emotion and cognition. As with all coactives, these are interlinked and interdependent, but each is a key factor in the performance of the player.

The term *spirituality* isn't exclusively about religious belief, although this can be an important part of a player's spiritual makeup. Spirituality involves an individual's identity, purpose in life and society, perceived role in society, community, team or tribe, and commitment to things they consider bigger than themselves.

Spirituality encompasses how players see themselves in relation to others. From time to time, players who struggle with relationship issues also struggle to relate to others in the locker room or have difficulties interacting with their coaches. The boundaries between personal and professional relationships are permeable and can't simply be dismissed as two distinct entities.

*Spirituality encompasses an individual's identity, purpose,
and perceived role in society.*

One's moral and ethical code underpins the spiritual coactive. Many young players have yet to find a goal for themselves or understand their place in life. This confusion often affects their ability to identify clear spiritual guidelines early on. The sooner they find this comfort, the easier it is for them to find peace in the perspectives and beliefs they hold.

Players with a strong spiritual center tend to better understand group dynamics and feel more confident about their role in the organization and in society. Someone who lacks this foundation often struggles in this regard. This doesn't have to be a matter of religious faith; a player may simply be out of sync with the spirit of the team and feel like an outsider who is not involved in the group dynamic.

For players to contribute and feel like part of a team, they must clearly identify a personal reason for why they come in every day and give their all. This is closely related to the player's needs and identity. There must be a connection on a spiritual level – a sense of belonging or a tangible power of togetherness.

It's essential that players have the sense that they are invested in the team and that their contributions are valued by the organization. This encourages a sense of responsibility and commitment:

- **Meaning:** Why am I doing this? Why are we doing this?
- **Connection:** What do I have to offer? What's expected of me?
- **Control:** How can I positively influence my performance and that of the team?

5.5.1.1   The Tribe

A team environment plays a major role on all the players associated with it. Being in a supportive, upbeat, and encouraging locker room can heighten players' feel-good hormones and suppress those hormones associated with perceived stress and negative emotions. Alternatively, negative energy can impact a tribe's psychology in a damaging way, with seemingly irrational and inexplicable actions of players or coaches who act out depressingly or aggressively. Negative energy can also be seen in the slumped shoulders and downward gazes of players whose teams have been playing badly, where the tribe has become collectively negative and pessimistic.

"It's definitely sustainable because when you treat men as men, and definitely keep the accountability high where there is no favoritism, there is no one person above the system; everybody is under the system, everybody is accountable, it just kind of keeps everybody in check. Everybody is leaning on you, you know everybody is expecting you to do your job and do it well. So, we have a bunch of great guys who have all bought into the system, too, and I haven't seen anybody fight the system, so it obviously works." [xvii]

- Defensive lineman Michael Brockers on Sean McVay's culture with the Los Angeles Rams

5.5.2   Emotion

Managing emotions on and off the field is an essential prerequisite for high performance and is arguably one of the most impactful components of psychological strength and ability. A player's decision-making process is partly reliant on past experiences and what he observes going on around him in the moment, but it's also closely tied to emotion.

A player's past and culture can affect emotional responses as well. Emotions are the fastest mechanisms in the body, so they have a great effect on players' actions and overall performance. How coaches and players communicate verbally and nonverbally sets the emotional context for each interaction. There's a hypocritical feeling when a coach constantly displays emotional outbursts and then scolds a player for drawing a penalty flag for acting the same way on the field.

The emotional environment that Bill Belichick creates for the New England Patriots has been described as "motivation through constant emotional discomfort," where the players learn to never flatline and keep a steady head when emotional situations arise during games. As such, the players learn not to panic when they perform poorly and not to get overly excited when they do well. In the end, execution is just about a job that needs to be done[xvii].

5.5.2.1   Out of Control

Often, when a player has emotional issues with teammates and/or coaches – such as irrational outbursts of anger during training exercises or oversensitivity to criticism – the source has little or nothing to do with the team environment. In many cases, players who struggle to make decisions on the field or within the organization have decision-making issues away from the game.

Stress can manifest itself in multiple areas of a player's life and wreak havoc on emotions. Addiction issues can manifest themselves powerfully in a player's emotions as well. So, if coaches are trying to help a player emotionally, they can look beyond what goes on during team activities and really pay attention to signs of psychological struggles. In certain cases, coaches may suggest professional psychological help if they are concerned about a player. People first, players second.

The ability to be considerate, compassionate, and empathetic is part of having **emotional intelligence** and is a necessary component for people to function well as part of a team.

Emotional intelligence is critical for:

- **Self-awareness**: Being mindful of feelings as they occur and how outward emotional display impacts others.
- **Managing emotions**: Accepting feelings as valid and appropriately finding ways to understand them.
- **Motivation**: Controlling emotions to focus, delay gratification, and limit impulsiveness.
- **Empathy**: Understanding others and recognizing that their emotions and feelings are valid.
- **Managing relationships**: Developing and maintaining healthy relationships.

5.5.2.3   The Confidence Game

There are two types of player confidence: external and internal. External confidence can come via feedback from a player's family, the media, fans, and other sources outside the team. The problem with external confidence is that it's built on shifting sands. The media can praise a team after one game and slam it after the next. Fans are similarly fickle as the season progresses. Even feedback from family members can vary daily.

The truest confidence is internal, where players and coaches determine the criteria by which they judge themselves and hold themselves to a high standard. How players feel about themselves as people shouldn't change based on the scoreboard or their stats, nor should they let external forces determine their sense of self-worth. It's certainly important to take constructive criticism from coaches and teammates, but it's equally important to be cautious of praise or derision from those outside of the organization.

5.5.3 Cognition

Cognition is the player's ability to focus, maintain attention, and mentally process what's going on during practice and games. Cognition encompasses information-processing, logical decision-making, studying the playbook, on-field awareness and critical thinking.

It's perfectly fine for coaches to expect a high-tempo, high-energy setting in practice, but they must also expect full cognitive commitment and concentration from players. Also, coaches can't lose sight of the cumulative cognitive load that players are experiencing throughout the week; such awareness ensures players can stay mentally fresh come game day.

> *We must expect full cognitive commitment and*
> *concentration from our players.*

The ability to focus and learn is profoundly impacted by stress and/or disruption to basic health. Being capable of engaging fully on the practice field, in the film room, or during supplemental learning scenarios, and then transferring these experiences to long-term memory is inextricably linked to a player's overall   well-being.

Conducting a basic psychological profile or having honest conversations with players and being mindful of areas like emotion, cognitive learning, and self-esteem allows coaches to clarify the areas of greatest need for psychological improvement:

- Does the player handle stress well?
- Is the player emotionally intelligent?
- Are there external issues affecting the player's mental and emotional state?
- Does the player process and learn information properly and fast enough?
- Does the player feel wanted and part of the team?
- Does the player feel appreciated?

5.5.3.1 How Players Learn Best

Constructing situations that expose players to realistic experiences allows them take ownership of their own learning, giving them the gift of independence and trust. Coaches could spend hours in front of a whiteboard diagramming plays, saying, "when player X moves here, you go there," but until they take these plays to the practice field and have players run through them, they really can't tell what they've absorbed.

The reality is that players are almost exclusively kinesthetic and visual in terms of how they learn. They learn by seeing and feeling their bodies act out motions in response to what they see – as diagrammed with the OODA loop. This is not necessarily because they were born with these learning preferences; rather, they have become the learning methods of choice through training and experience. This means that they learn best by operating in situations that mirror the game as closely as possible.

Coaches can help players not by telling them what to do all the time, but by setting up learning opportunities that enable them to figure it out for themselves. The more realistic the practice situation, the more seamlessly the players will apply their learned habits in games. The task is to plan sessions as efficiently as possible so that players spend less time listening to instructions and more time learning to respond to game situations.

5.5.3.2   Tapping into the Subconscious

During practice, instead of trying to explain every detail of every drill, it is more important to focus on very specific verbal instructions and then let the players go through the experience and figure out what they're supposed to do on their own. Practice time is very limited so it's important for players to have quality experiences, not listen to talk the whole time.

Allowing players to explore solutions will engage their subconscious mind, meaning they won't be as self-conscious or stressed out. A clear head will let them figure out the best way to execute the skills for the learning scenario. This set-up is far more effective than having a preconceived idea of how skills should be performed and stopping practice every time a player improvises.

We want to prioritize quality experiences

When really thinking about it, if a quarterback gets the ball to the right receiver, then he made the play. Should coaches spend time nit-picking his technique? Bringing up too many issues will only lead to **paralysis by analysis** – giving the players so many things to think about that they end up overloaded and frozen in confusion. So, it is less about repetition of exact movements and instead about repetition of experiences.

If a quarterback struggles to find a receiver when facing pressure, coaches can recreate a high-pressure experience in practice for him and encourage him to find a successful solution. Allowing him to get creative against different experiences will make him a far more confident player, engraining positive habits that are psychologically positive. He now feels like he has ownership of his own development.

Coaches are better off spending time constructing the right learning experience to facilitate a particular outcome than explaining at length to the player what the goal is, which element it relates to, and so on. All the player needs to know is the situation and how to respond to scenarios.

5.5.3.3   Weekly Psychological Considerations

The traditional focus in football is on developing physical qualities like strength, power, speed, and endurance. But, in our opinion, the weekly cycle we propose is more effective because it recognizes the body and brain as one, considering the combination of mental and physical loads.

Players may have long blocks of concentration that are high in volume, such as a long day of film review, walk-throughs, and meetings. Then there are activities that are psychologically demanding and intensive, like learning new plays or techniques. These sessions require greater cognitive recovery than sessions that take less of a mental toll on players.

> *Learning new plays or techniques is psychologically*
> *demanding and intensive*

Brain-demanding activities can also take a tremendous physical toll on a person from a total stress perspective – consider a stockbroker who suddenly dies of a heart attack.

The point is, coaches can't merely look at the practice week through a physical lens without also considering the week's psychological implications. It is necessary to think about the total stress load on the body and how to help players manage this load.

5.6   The Physical Coactive

In this section, we hope to explain the concepts around a player's physical traits and how they are interrelated with the other coactives. We'll go over some the various components of physical skills and how to express and develop them.

5.6.1   Movement and Motion

We do not wish to dive into a deep theoretical argument as it relates to what movement really is. There are literally hundreds of books that attempt to tackle this issue, and several highly intelligent people who continue to disagree on various aspects of movement and motion. Some of these are listed in the resources section at the back of this book.

Instead, we hope to give a very simple overview of some of the terms found in strength and conditioning and sports science, and what they mean for physically developing players.

5.6.1.1   Biomechanics – Understanding Movement with Physics

Biomechanics encompass both the physical positions and movements of a player as well as the forces that cause those movements. The study of **kinematics** considers body positions and observation of movement without reference to what caused the movement to occur. Kinematics deal with the observable *shape* a player portrays during motion as well as the acceleration or velocity of motion. Some coaches, like our friends at ALTIS, always ask: what shape is most efficient for the specific athlete and specific situation?

In contrast, the term **kinetics** is used when studying the forces that went into making that motion possible. Newton's laws of physics explain that any initiation or change of motion will require force. So, take any physical performance quality, whether it be strength, power, speed, endurance, or even mobility, and understand that force must be generated for movement to occur.

Kinematics and kinetics come together when observing how force interacts with aspects of velocity and time. When talking about a player having a lot of power, what's really being said is that he has a great combination of force and velocity. Some sport actions will not allow for a lot of time, like having to quickly cut around an opponent, and force will be time dependent. So, one may observe how much force a player can exhibit when time is a performance constraint.

Biomechanics allow one to observe the outputs of how the nervous system, hormonal (endocrine) system, energy systems, and the muscular system come together to manifest expressions of physical performance. Sports science is heavily fixated upon biomechanics, measuring how powerful a player is, how much force he generates, his maximum sprinting velocity, and other similar measurements.

Biomechanics set the functional foundation of a player and how he moves. It's not just related to the fixed capabilities of joints and tissues, but also to global aspects of mobility and the brain's ability to coordinate the body structures and segments into action. Using a biomechanical approach, one can start asking questions related to shapes and skills.

5.6.1.1.1 Are Our Players Strong Enough?

By combining knowledge of biomechanics with a thorough understanding of the football Game Model, coaches can assess a player's physical prowess as it relates to his game performance. From this vantage point, strength really refers to how well the players can apply force and achieve a specific outcome when faced with various movement constraints.[xix]

This means that strength is not just about how much weight a player can squat or bench press. For strength to be analyzed in terms of its usefulness for football performance, coaches and scouts must consider the task requirements of each player's position and the constraints they will face when playing the game.

The first stop when questioning if a player is strong enough is to evaluate film from practice and games. Does he play strong? If scouts see a player getting tossed around the field and unable to stay on his feet, then they can say he does not play strong. They then work backwards from the film and determine why he is struggling.

Perhaps it's not really a strength issue. Maybe the player does not understand what to do from a tactical perspective or is operating with poor technical execution. Or he may not possess enough mobility and flexibility to achieve the required technical positions to play strong.

The reason strength and conditioning coaches have players lift weights is to help them learn to generate force from a general perspective. The weight room is a very controlled environment, meaning that coaches can expose players to large amounts of force in a way that is safe (with proper coaching) and leads to desirable physical adaptations.

The resistance exercises in the weight room help players adapt by teaching them how to coordinate their nervous systems to activate larger percentages of muscle mass at faster rates, producing higher amounts of force. In addition, resistance exercises will develop players from a structural standpoint, leading to increased muscle mass (hypertrophy), improving the integrity of connective tissues like the tendons and ligaments, and improving bone density.

While weight room strength plays a fundamental role in a complete physical preparation program, coaches still must place it in its proper context. Some players may not exhibit great strength in the weight room but will certainly play strong on the field.

Safety Tyrann Mathieu is a wonderful example of this point. Mathieu went to the 2013 NFL Combine and was criticized for only achieving four repetitions on the 225-pound bench press test, raising questions about his work ethic as it related to off-season strength training.[xx]

In ironic fashion, these same critics likely also acknowledge how meaningless the bench press test is in terms of analyzing a player's skill set. Indeed, for anyone who decides to view Mathieu's game film from his time at Louisiana State University, it quickly becomes apparent that the 186-pound, "undersized" defensive back has the capability to explode into blockers and take ball carriers off their feet, certainly showing aspects of playing strong.

So, while coaches want to see players continue to improve in the weight room from a force-production standpoint, they can keep everything in context by observing how players are operating in the game before deciding that strength is a true limitation.

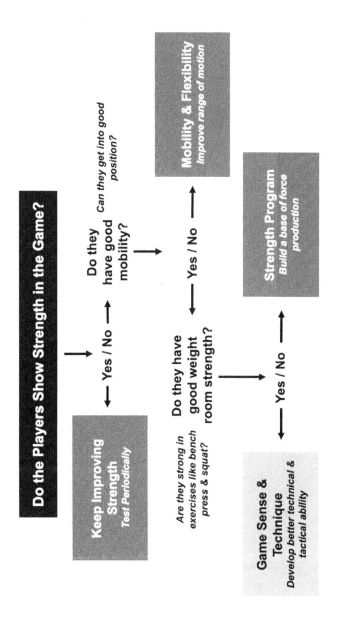

5.6.1.1.2   Are Our Players Fast Enough?

Speed is an interesting paradox as it relates to football. Most college football coaches would agree that they desperately want to recruit speed, even going so far as to question high school players on their involvement in track and field. In fact, many players are overlooked simply because they *don't* participate in track and field. If a player chooses not to participate in track and field, then he had better make sure he can find a way to get a verified 40-yard-dash time so that coaches are aware of how fast he is. We live in a time where numbers sometimes seem to be more important than what a coach can see with his own eyes.

In truth, coaches don't need a 40-yard or 100-meter sprint time to tell them if a player can play fast football. All he needs to do is put on some film and watch how the player plays the game. To be fair, there is no question that a player who can run a fast sprint time will have the *potential* to play fast football. Still, the fact remains: a player's sprint time will tell coaches almost nothing about what kind of football player he is. In contrast, game film will show scouts exactly how the player operates in a game environment.

Some high school and college players will show some nice flash on film but play in a league that isn't very competitive, making it tougher to distinguish how these players will function at higher levels of competition. For this purpose, football camps are valuable as coaches can invite players to participate in football-related exercises with other highly touted prospects and see how they perform.

Measuring a 40-yard-dash can help, but its value is as an objective analysis in combination with subjective indicators from watching a player play football. Some prospects may have never run a 40-yard-dash and may not test well. These same prospects may show great awareness and skill when it comes to competitive football exercises like 7-on-7 games.

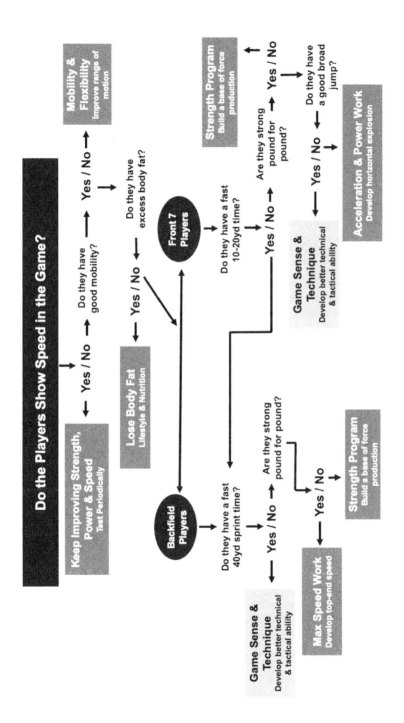

Do the Players Show Speed in the Game?

Keep Improving Strength, Power & Speed
Test Periodically

Yes / No → Do they have good mobility? → Yes / No →

Mobility & Flexibility
Improve range of motion

Do they have excess body fat?

Yes / No →

Lose Body Fat
Lifestyle & Nutrition

Front 7 Players

Do they have a fast 10-20yd time? → Yes / No →

Game Sense & Technique
Develop better technical & tactical ability

Are they strong pound for pound? → Yes / No →

Strength Program
Build a base of force production

Do they have a good broad jump? → Yes / No →

Acceleration & Power Work
Develop horizontal explosion

Backfield Players

Do they have a fast 40yd sprint time? → Yes / No →

Max Speed Work
Develop top-end speed

Are they strong pound for pound? → Yes / No →

Strength Program
Build a base of force production

Game Sense & Technique
Develop better technical & tactical ability

As with everything else, the first step of analysis is to look at the game and work backwards from there. Scouts might ignore a player who doesn't have a good 40-yard-dash time, only to watch him go play for a conference opponent and cause trouble for the team that did not recruit him for years to come. Or, scouts might get excited about signing the player who runs a 4.3-second 40-yard-dash and later get frustrated because he struggles to translate this speed into playing fast football.

The reality is that game-related speed is far more complex than what is devised from a 40-yard-dash test. Great players understand when to slow things down and when to burst into another gear, all of which is dictated by what they are perceiving in the game environment. While having access to a lot of speed will always be an asset, being able to use that speed in an effective manner when playing football is the better indicator of success.

Sometimes there are players who have all the raw speed in the world but will not be very successful until they improve their game sense and technique. Other times there are players who understand the game very well and need more physical development to get their speed where it needs to be. Looking at the big picture will help coaches understand which route to take in ensuring their players are fast enough.

5.6.1.1.3   Adding Context to Biomechanics

Back to the common theme: biomechanics must be understood in context. Coaches must form their own judgments whether a player's game performance reflects a shortcoming in some physical output before going crazy over any objective data. That said, when a limitation is physical in nature, the measurements and data obtained from a sport science staff are incredibly valuable to help players progress. This is especially true when players are coming back from injury and are being assessed for their return-to-play status.

5.6.1.2   Bioenergetics – Fueling Movement

Bioenergetics concern the body's energy systems and how they provide a player with cellular fuel during training and competition. Here, the concern lies in the ability of these systems to distribute energy substrates and oxygenated blood to the working muscles for sustained work. One must also account for the muscles' ability to utilize these substrates once they are transported locally.

Bioenergetic capacity is commonly understood as "conditioning," although this word by itself is very non-descriptive. Conditioning can come in various forms and is based on the necessary requirements of a sport task. For example, the conditioning of an Olympic weightlifter is very different than the conditioning of a marathon runner, yet both may be considered "in shape" for their sports.

5.6.1.2.1   Harnessing Energy

To provide the fuel required for different types of work, the body uses two broad energy system pathways: **aerobic** energy metabolism and **anaerobic** energy metabolism, the latter having two sub-systems discussed soon. At *no* time is any one energy system operating in isolation.

During exercise and movement, the body will find ways to energize action by calling upon all the energy systems, in differing degrees, depending on the specific task at hand. This provides the body with cellular fuel (known as adenosine-triphosphate or ATP) to power activity. The more fuel delivered to working structures, and the better the cells can utilize this fuel, the more work can be sustained.

When it comes to understanding the necessary "conditioning" for any sport, coaches must consider the following three points:

Rate of Energy Production (Power)

How much power do athletes need to generate and how quickly must power be displayed? Sports that require frequent explosive movement will require much higher rates of energy production in comparison to endurance-based sports.

Duration of Energy Production (Capacity)

How long will athletes need to maintain power output over a sustained period? Endurance-based sports will require athletes to maintain moderate levels of power over very long periods of time, which differs from intermittent team sports or power-based sports like sprinting, jumping, and Olympic weightlifting, where high levels of power are put on display for relatively short periods of time.

Work-to-Rest Ratio

How much rest will athletes have between bouts of continuous activity? An intermittent team sport like football will feature explosive movement for around 5-10 seconds followed by a recovery period of 20-40 seconds between plays, resulting in a work-to-rest ratio of about 1:4. In contrast, endurance-based sports like running a marathon will have no rest at all, with continuous work being performed for hours.

5.6.1.2.2   The Aerobic System

Aerobic metabolism is the most efficient form of energy utilization and is the primary energy system used for long-duration work. Aerobic processes can break down stored carbohydrates and fat, yielding the greatest quantity of cellular fuel (ATP). However, the aerobic system requires oxygen and many chemical steps in the process of yielding usable energy, which requires a relatively long time to obtain. For immediate, explosive activities of high intensity, the body needs more immediate energy resources obtained from anaerobic metabolism. Therefore, we consider football to be an anaerobic sport by nature.

That said, aerobic metabolism plays a part in replenishing energy substrates during the rest periods following activities of high intensity. In theory, after a few minutes of game activity, the aerobic system is activated and given a window of time in between plays to grab some oxygen and start replenishing energy resources. When players have better aerobic fitness, this process can happen sooner and more efficiently.[xx]

5.6.1.2.3   The Anaerobic System

Anaerobic metabolism provides working cells with fuel at a much faster rate than aerobic metabolism, which is necessary for explosive performance. The trade-off is that the amount of total energy utilized is much less than what the aerobic system provides, about six percent of the energy as molecules of ATP (two molecules versus thirty-six molecules). However, if players have adequate aerobic development, energy can be replenished in between bouts of high-intensity activity, allowing for continued energy available for explosive action.

Anaerobic metabolism has two sub-systems: the **anaerobic glycolytic (lactic)** system and the **anaerobic phosphagen (alactic)** system. For sake of simplicity, we will refer to these as the lactic and alactic systems. Without turning this into a physiology lesson, the lactic system is the primary energy system utilized during high-intensity activity of relatively longer durations (about 30 seconds to 2 minutes) and the alactic system is primarily utilized during high-intensity activity of very short durations (less than 30 seconds).

Football has commonly been described as an alactic-aerobic sport. It would take a very rare play to go beyond a duration of thirty seconds, so it's easy to understand that the alactic system is the primary energy pathway used in football. The aerobic component is in reference to the replenishment of energy substrates between bouts of alactic activity.

However, when teams decide to go at a fast tempo, there will be minimal rest time between plays, making high-intensity action more continuous and the lactic system more dominant. Thus, players must be prepared to deal with differing situations, so they cannot pigeon-hole into any one energy system. If properly developed using realistic game scenarios, the energy systems will function as desired for game play.

5.6.1.2.4   Adding Context to Conditioning

Coaches often blame poor conditioning as a major limiting factor of game performance, which is a very narrow-minded notion. Again, it's not about conditioning for the sake of conditioning - it's about finding actual limiting factors of performance and determining how to condition those aspects.

A player's body need only fuel him for the sport tasks found in the game context. Just because a player can run 300-yard shuttles all day long tells nothing about how effectively he can operate in a football game for four quarters. Work capacity and endurance are very specific; a champion triathlete can't be expected to dominate a football game.

A player is "in shape" when he can sustain high football performance throughout practice and throughout games. For coaching purposes, players must have the capacity to carry out the playbook, keep up with opponents, and operate effectively within the confines of the game over four quarters of play.

"The biggest mistake is to increase an athlete's ability to produce force or power without also developing the capacity for increased energy

production that's necessary to use it within the physical demands of their sport."

- Joel Jamieson, 8 Weeks Out

5.6.2   Anthropometrics – Body Size, Structure, and Shape

The size and proportion of every player's body is largely determined by heredity – that is, their underlying genetic make-up. While heredity will govern height, bone structure, ratio of limb length to torso length, body type, body shape, and so on, body *composition* can be manipulated through activity and nutrition, such as increasing a player's muscle mass or decreasing his body fat percentage.

5.6.2.1   Body Structure & Biomechanics

A player's body structure will dictate his biomechanical experience. Two players may squat the same amount of weight, but if one is a lanky, six-foot-three wide receiver and the other is a compact, five-foot-nine running back, their experiences during the lift will be very different. The ranges of motion, the compression on the joints, the intermuscular coordination, and many other factors will differ, despite similar outputs in measured performance.

How a player's body structures align also influences the intensity of movement. Mobility work, massage, and chiropractic therapy can help re-align internal structures like muscles, bones, and fascia so that nerves aren't impinged and are better able to send impulses to muscles. This nerve-signaling is a key determinant of how much power output is available and usable. Maintaining structural integrity will also help ensure fluidity and nutrient transport to the tissues through improved blood flow and reduced connective tissue viscosity.

All players must have a baseline of mobility allowing them to get into the proper shapes for the positions they play. A lineman that doesn't have the mobility to get into an efficient stance will have poor leverage against his opponent and risk losing a lot of potential power. If players lack this baseline capacity, they will struggle to stabilize their bodies and rely on sub-optimal compensation patterns, putting them in riskier positions that wreak havoc on their body structures. This can lead to more restriction and less range of motion over time.

Players must have a baseline of mobility allowing them to
get into the proper shapes for the positions they play.

In addition to achieving the shapes of their football position, players should have the capacity to exhibit shapes associated with a fully functional human being.

Body structure and body function are inseparable qualities. Poor mobility can impact structural integrity when tight tissues and compromised positions start causing damage, leading to structural degeneration over time. Structure also impacts mobility and some players may have a structural predisposition to achieve certain positions more easily than others. The key is to obtain enough mobility to maximize the potential of inherited body structure while moving in a sustainable manner that does not harm body tissues.

5.6.3   Determining Limiting Factors

To the extent possible, coaches must find the limiting factors holding a player back from improving his performance on the field. A mistake often made is assuming that if players can lift twenty more pounds or withstand another four repetitions of 110-yard sprints, they will magically improve on game day. The problem with this approach is that it's essentially just guess work, often leading to overtraining and under-performance.

A far better approach is to use the Game Model to identify the true limiting factors of player performance in the context of the game. This way, coaches can clearly see if players need to improve certain physical qualities and they can devise a plan to get there.

FACTORS AFFECTING GAME PERFORMANCE
Identifying & Reducing Limiting Factors

Technical-Tactical	Body Composition	Movement Coordination	Movement Execution	Neuromuscular & Motor Performance	Biological & Energy System Performance	Psychological & Sensory Factors	Lifestyle & Nutrition	Training Variables
Understanding of Game Plan	Body Fat	General Movement Coordination	Shin Angle During Acceleration	Maximum Strength (Overcome Force)	Short Term Energy (Alactic Power & Capacity)	Spirituality (Sense of Place in the World)	Sleep Quality	Allostatic Load (Total Stress Load)
Effective Skill Execution	Muscle Mass	Ability to Actively Dorsiflex on Ground Contact	Trunk Rotation When Sprinting	Isometric Strength (Resist Force)	Intermediate Energy (Anaerobic Power & Capacity)	Personal Value System	Hydration	Volume of Training
Decision-Making in Sport	Tension in the Hips & Lower Legs	Trunk Control When Running at High Speeds	Position of Center of Mass When Changing Direction	Eccentric Strength (Yield to Force)	Long-Term Energy (Aerobic Power & Capacity)	General Thoughts & Feelings	Anti-Inflammatory Food Ingestion	Intensity of Training
Perception (Field Awareness)	Tension in the Shoulders & Lower Arms	Muscle Tension-Relaxation Coordination	Position of Center of Mass When Entering Collision	Power with High Force (Strength-Speed)	Local Muscular Endurance	Vision & Hearing (Can You See & Hear Properly?)	Stimulant Ingestion	Density of Training
Sport Situational Awareness	Tension in the Jaw & Neck	Ability to Quickly "Stop & Go"	Position of Base of Support in Multiple Movement Planes	Power with High Velocity (Speed-Strength)	Breathing Patterns	Perception of Stress	Supplementation Ingestion	Collision in Training
Game Experience	Active Joint Range of Motion	Ability to Explode & Accelerate Off Both Feet	Body Positioning in 360 Degrees of Movement	Mechanical Stiffness During Elastic Actions (Spring)	Stress Response (Heart Rate Variability)	Emotional Intelligence & Self-Awareness	Drug & Alcohol Use	CNS Stimulation (Magnitude & Frequency)
Game Communication	Spinal Mechanics (Neutral Spine)			Momentum (Product of Body Mass & Acceleration)	Inflammatory Response (Soreness, Aching)	Addiction Issues	Under- or Over-Eating	Recovery Protocols
				Trunk Strength & Strength Endurance	Glycogen Levels	Ability to Focus & Avoid Distraction		

It's also necessary to understand that physical development is not limited to the strength and conditioning sessions. Practice is a form of physical training, so coaches can address limiting factors related to physical shortcomings in practice activities as well.

In fact, by understanding the Four-Coactive Model, the strength staff and football staff can work together in a coherent way to determine which physical qualities will be addressed in practice and which will be addressed in the strength and conditioning sessions. This is a perfect example of letting the game guide the preparation process throughout the organization.

Coaches also need to determine if the issue is in fact physical. or if it's a limitation due to one of the other coactives. If they find that it is indeed a physical issue, then it becomes a matter of figuring out the root of the problem, determining the best exercise or method to solve it, and then setting aside time before, during, or after practice for the player to work on it.

The truth is that most physical limitations are related to coordination and skill. As track and field coaches like Dan Pfaff and Stu McMillan have discussed, one reason that sprinters are able to continue getting faster is that they refine the skill-oriented aspects of their technique consistently, all year long. For this reason, sometimes improvements in speed can come from focusing on technical points, even if the actual speeds experienced in training are submaximal.

The same can be said of weightlifters or powerlifters who find ways to get stronger by using submaximal weights, intentionally performing each lift as skillfully as possible. Many of the best Olympic weightlifters use a small percentage of their annual training loads with maximum weight; the rest of the year is spent honing technique with lighter loads.

So, even when a limitation is considered "physical," like a lack of strength or speed, players will need to have the right mindset, technique, and executional understanding for a squat, bench press, sprint, jump, or any other exercise.

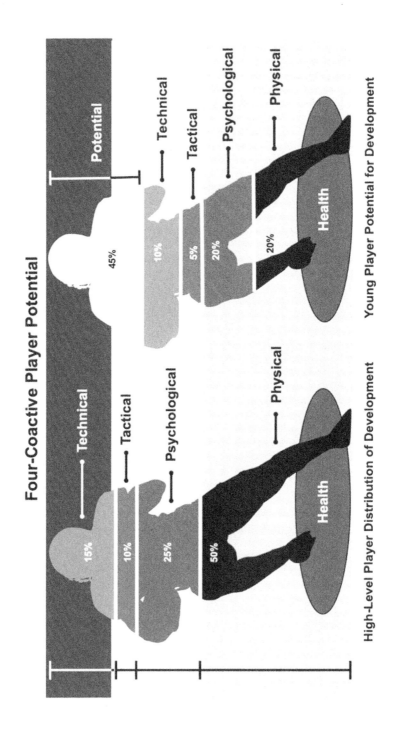

Four-Coactive Player Potential

Potential

Technical — 45%

Technical — 10%

Tactical — 5%

Psychological — 20%

Physical — 20%

Health

Young Player Potential for Development

Technical — 15%

Tactical — 10%

Psychological — 25%

Physical — 50%

Health

High-Level Player Distribution of Development

5.6.4 Physical Performance Qualities

Below we present different physical performance qualities that contribute to movement execution during various skills and exercises. The qualities discussed are not all-encompassing and there is an extensive range of classified physical qualities in sport training literature; we have simply provided what we feel is an overview of the ones most commonly named.

It's important to note that none of these qualities exist in isolation; they are collectively involved all the time in varying degrees of proportionality depending upon the task being performed. Again, physical development does not only occur with a strength and conditioning coach. Football practice is inherently physical and can be strategically used to develop physical abilities that are fully specific to game performance.

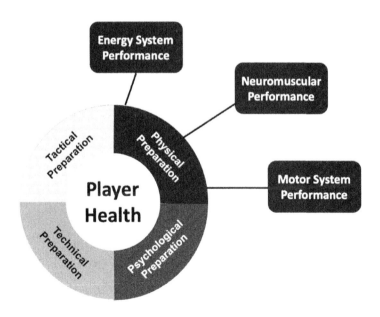

5.6.4.1 Energy System Performance Qualities

The energy system performance qualities are in direct reference to the functionality of the aerobic and anaerobic systems. Energy system performance is specific to the task at hand, so the best results will be obtained when training these qualities as they will be used when players are on the field.

Most college football teams have a conditioning test before the start of camp, like running sixteen 110-yard sprints or performing two series of 300-yard shuttles. The players are challenged to arrive at camp "in shape" to pass these tests and are considered "out of shape" if they don't pass. However, coaches must always ask themselves this question: in shape for what?

While players are preparing for their 300-yard shuttle test over the summer, positive physical changes are definitely happening: the heart will start to pump blood more efficiently, the blood vessels improve delivery of nutrients and exchanging of by-products, and the local musculature becomes better able to harness energy substrates.

But, how usable will these adaptations be for the specific actions of playing football? If coaches only prepare players with 300-yard shuttles, then they will only be "in shape" for 300-yard shuttles.

ENERGY SYSTEM PERFORMANCE QUALITIES

	Alactic Power	Alactic Capacity	Anaerobic Power	Anaerobic Capacity	Aerobic Power	Aerobic Capacity
Typical Work-to-Rest Ratio	1:10	1:6	1:4	1:2	1:1	1:<1
Explanation	The most rapid energy system; capable of the highest outputs of power over very brief durations. typically <10 secs	The ability to sustain the highest outputs of power over very brief durations with some fatigue.	The ability to perform high intensity movements over various distances for relatively short durations.	The ability to sustain high intensity outputs & relatively explosive actions as larger amounts of fatigue start to accumulate.	The ability to operate effectively in game as the highest amounts of fatigue begin to set in. The highest sustainable power output over long durations of work with little or no rest.	The ability to continue performing work for as long as necessary - based upon aerobic capacity & the replenishment of fuel sources.
Example(s) in Football	Present in any major explosive movement on the field – jumping for a catch, tackling a ball carrier, drive blocking an opponent off the ball, rapidly changing direction, or sprinting	The primary energy system of football due to the requirement of performing repeated brief, explosive activity over the course of a drive with incomplete rest intervals (20-40 secs) between plays.	Density of football drives typically constitute 1-2 plays a minute when stoppages do not occur - helps fuel player as drives continue for more than one play without stoppage.	A long drive where a team utilizes a slow ball style of play will require players to have enough capacity to continue operating at high intensity for up to 10-12 consecutive plays.	Exemplified when a running back breaks a big run after already carrying the ball several times on a drive or when a pass rusher can get a sack after being on the field for several consecutive plays.	Highly relevant during long sustained drives of fast ball style of play - up-tempo, up to 3-4 plays per minute. It is also indicative of the ability to continue operating over the course of a full game.
Development in Sports Practice	Developed when players are encouraged to perform brief, explosive actions in practice with full recovery between bouts.	Developed in individual periods of practice when players are challenged to perform more consecutive explosive actions with incomplete rest.	Emphasized in technical-tactical drills in individual & unit periods of practice, focusing on high intensity efforts with longer intervals of rest.	Developed during tactical games or small-sided games where 3 rotating teams are used & rep counts are lower.	Developed during tactical games or small-sided games where 2 rotating teams are used & rep counts are higher.	Results from the summation effect of all other forms of practice.
Development in Strength & Conditioning	Developed using explosive activities like sprinting, plyometrics, jumping, & brief high-intensity weight training (1-2 reps) with full recovery between sets.	Developed using explosive activities as part of a complex. Acceleration complexes or power circuits are common.	Developed using heavy resistance training where time under tension falls between 30-60s of work (i.e. 5-6 reps) with full recovery between sets.	Developed using tempo running intervals, strength endurance & hypertrophy in the weight room.	Developed using extensive intervals of activity where the time of work is the same as the rest time (1:1 ratio)	Developed by performing bouts of activity with very low rest, for example 60s of work followed by 30s rest.

119

General exercises may be useful to achieve desired physical adaptations. But to truly impact game performance, physical preparation must also include preparation activities that are game-like, where the OODA loop is present, and players are dealing with cognitive fatigue in conjunction with physical fatigue.

As we will discuss later, the use of physical education games in the off-season, as well as carefully constructed football practices in-season, can both accomplish this aim.

5.6.4.2   Neuromuscular Performance Qualities

The term **neuromuscular** describes the interacting relationship between the nervous system (neuro-) and muscular system. For our purposes, we will give a small overview of the primary muscular contractions coordinated by the nervous system.

These different contractions are also understood as regimes of muscular work, whereby the muscles are activated for overcoming resistance (concentric), withstanding resistance (eccentric), resisting motion by matching the force of resistance (isometric), and taking advantage of reflexes and stored energy from the tendons to power rapid, explosive movement (elastic).

5.6.4.3   Motor System Performance Qualities

The motor system performance qualities are in reference to the observable outputs associated with performance in sport. Here we are primarily concerned with movement power as well as the capacity to sustain movement.

Power is the product of force and velocity, so various athletic maneuvers will require different combinations of strength and speed. In some cases, more force will be needed to handle higher resistances and in other cases more speed will be necessary to execute quickly. In addition, some actions will require sustained outputs associated with strength while other actions require sustained outputs associated with speed.

NEUROMUSCULAR PERFORMANCE QUALITIES

	Concentric Strength (Overcoming)	Isometric Strength (Resisting)	Eccentric Strength (Yielding)	Elastic Strength (Reacting)
Explanation	The ability to generate a maximal singular application of force. Commonly understood as how much resistance a player can overcome.	The ability to use muscular force to resist motion. Characterized by generating high force with very little to no outward movement.	The ability to use muscular force to absorb external forces. Eccentric force absorption, such as making a cut when changing direction, is very high during rapid force absorption.	The ability to perform rapid, explosive actions using "free energy" from other connective tissues like tendons in stretch-shortening cycle. Players with great elastic strength will appear smooth & springy while moving.
Example(s) in Football	Situations that include collision (blocking or tackling). Generally, the closer a player's position to the ball before the snap, the greater requirement of concentric strength. Also necessary for acceleration & explosive actions.	An offensive lineman holds his ground against a bull rush from a defensive tackle, staying anchored. Perimeter players set the edge & hold contain against fast flowing outside attacks.	When a lineman drives into the man across from him, he must first absorb his opponent's force before overcoming it. Any time a player changes direction, he must first absorb the external forces acting against his intended direction of movement before successfully redirecting.	Important for speed positions that typically portray high movement speeds & vertical jumping efforts – namely wide receivers & defensive backs. When skill players have great elastic ability, they will use less energy from muscles, spreading force across other connective tissues & improving stamina as well as lowering risk of muscle strain.
Development in Sports Practice	Developed in practice activities where players collide with one another, accelerate quickly over very short distances (i.e. 5-10yds), or perform jumping actions (i.e. high point catching, goal line fades)	Developed in practice situations that emphasize collision will develop isometric strength due to the intent of not giving up ground.	Developed during practice activities that require frequent changes of direction as well as collision in the form of tackling or blocking dummies or opponents.	Developed on plays with longer sprinting efforts & where players must leave the ground to go up for the football, such as a goal line fade.
Development in Strength & Conditioning	Developed using resistance training with high loads, particularly loads close to a player's one-repetition maximum (1RM). Concentric strength is typically synonymous with a player's maximum strength.	Developed in multiple ways, either by performing exercises that hold positions for minimal time (3-6s) against high loads or extended time (30-60s) against low loads, or where force is applied to an immovable object, like pressing a barbell into safety pins.	Developed in multiple ways, each posing unique specificity. Emphasize eccentric control with slow tempo during absorption phase or using supramaximal loads (>100% 1RM) where the lifter is assisted on the way up or uses special equipment to unload the concentric phase. High eccentric force is also present during rapid force absorption, like the catch phase of an Olympic lift or using flywheel training devices.	Developed using rapid, explosive exercises like sprinting, plyometrics & depth jumps with minimal ground contact time (<0.25s). Best emphasized in lighter players, since heavier players will experience a greater risk of connective tissue trauma with elastic loading due to higher gravitational resistance of their own body weight.

MOTOR SYSTEM PERFORMANCE QUALITIES

	Power (Explosiveness)	Strength-Speed	Speed-Strength	Elastic Stiffness (Reactive Ability)	Strength Endurance	Speed Endurance
Explanation	The product of force & velocity (strength & speed). Associated with the rate of force development (RFD). The ability to exert force quickly. Any explosive activity encompasses power.	Applying power where strength is more important than speed due to substantial resistance. Force outweighs velocity for product of power.	Applying power where speed is more important than strength. The ability to accelerate & achieve top speed (or close to it) & hold it for a short time. Velocity outweighs force for product of power.	The ability to exert large amounts of power in a rapid manner after a sharp mechanical stretching of the connective tissues by an external force.	The ability to apply strength over an extended period or several times in quick succession.	The ability to generate speed & either sustain it in a continuous effort or reproduce it several times in succession.
Example(s) in Football	All things equal, the player who can operate faster than his opponent will be more powerful in the context of the game. It might not be the player with the most absolute power that is most successful, but the player who can use power most effectively.	Any time a player collides with an opponent, there is substantial resistance to overcome. In addition, it's not just about moving the opponent, but moving him quickly & explosively, a major indicator of a player's strength-speed.	Speed-strength is on display when a running back finds an open crease & bursts into the end zone or when a free safety reads a deep throw entering this zone, sprinting to get to the ball & intercept it.	Elastic stiffness is a very important physical quality for positions operating at high speeds. All players will require aspects of elastic stiffness for rapid changes of direction.	No matter the position, collision is going to occur for all players. Having a solid foundation of strength & the work capacity to display it repeatedly will help ensure that collisions are not as fatiguing.	Increasing a player's maximum speed will raise his 'operational speed', that is, reduce the amount of effort it will take him to run to different areas of the field. If a player is fast & also technically & tactically sound, he will display great speed endurance.
Development in Sports Practice	Developed any time players perform explosive actions in practice.	Practice situations featuring intense changes of direction or collision will develop game-related strength-speed.	Developed in the context of the game with practice situations where players are encouraged to operate with effective acceleration, not necessarily as fast as possible where they might lose control.	Developed by exposing players to high-speed situations in the context of the game as well as using drills & games requiring speed players to time jumps properly when playing the ball.	Developed by exposing players to a calculated volume of collision-based activities which will help improve their usable strength endurance in the game context.	Developed by challenging players in drills & games to operate at high speeds repeatedly over multiple plays & series of plays.
Development in Strength & Conditioning	Developed using sprints, jumps, plyometrics, explosive throws, Olympic lifting & velocity-based training.	Using Olympic lifts develops strength-speed due to power against substantial loads. Explosive jumps & throws are other examples where players must project their own bodies or a medicine ball into space for height or distance.	Developed using linear acceleration & speed drills as well as putting a focus on the use of games in the off-season to help players learn to combine acceleration with perception & action.	Developed by using high-speed sprinting as well as plyometric exercises like skips, hops, bounds & depth jumps. Change of direction activities can help players learn to understand how to apply biomechanical principles like lowering the center of mass when cutting to be more stable.	Any training activity that uses moderately heavy resistance for higher volumes of work will develop strength endurance.	Developed using acceleration complexes or other forms of repeated sprint ability (RSA). In addition, the use of intensive small-sided games in the off-season will give more information as to how a player can organize this operational speed in a game setting.

5.6.5   The Most Important Factor for Sustainable Success

Hands down, player health is the most important physical factor for achieving maximal and sustained performance. Coaches are not interested in winning one game or going through one successful season...they're interested in dominating and winning *multiple* championships. For that, the health of their players is essential.

One of the main goals of the Four-Coactive Model is to enable players to continue making small improvements every day and, ultimately, for these advances to result in more wins. For this to come to fruition, coaches must maintain the overall health of their players as best as possible, especially with busy training schedules.

Physical health is a key factor in its own right – players need to be physically fit to play their best. But, it's also a precursor to achieving balance in the body's chemistry, which has a positive impact on player mental states as well. A player who leads an unbalanced, unhealthy lifestyle might be able to cheat biology for a time. But after a while, the cracks will widen into canyons and the player will fall through. Talk to most NFL players who have ended their careers earlier than expected and they will say, "I wish I had taken better care of my body."

> *A player who leads an unbalanced, unhealthy lifestyle*
> *might be able to cheat biology...but only for a time.*

While it is the responsibility of the player to take care of himself, the coaching staff, medical team, strength and conditioning staff, sports science staff, and other members of an organization also have a moral and ethical duty to look after players. Health is more than just eating right, getting enough sleep, and avoiding excessive drinking or drug use.

For example, trying to attain mental toughness by beating players down physically, day in and day out, seeing if they can overcome it, poses a very high risk to their health. Similarly, when berating a player verbally and trying to break him down psychologically through insult and mental manipulation, the damage might not show at first, but the health of that player is likely being sacrificed from the inside-out.

6 Player Health

Health is often viewed through a black and white lens: a player is either healthy or he isn't. But this is incorrect, as every person's health falls along a continuum. Teams run into potential problems when assuming players are only "unhealthy" if they're sick or injured.

The contention is to no longer look at player health as simply "sick/not sick," or "injured/ not injured" binary oppositions. Instead, coaches owe it to their players to start thinking about their health holistically and with a broader perspective, rather than just worrying about how many games or practices an individual is going to miss.

The corollary is also true: 99 percent healthy is not 100 percent injured. In other words, just because a player might be a little beat up does not mean there is nothing for him to do. There is always *something* a player can do, even if he has a broken leg.

Player preparation far exceeds physical measures, so even if a player is severely limited from a physical standpoint, he can prepare himself psychologically and tactically by learning playbook concepts and becoming a student of the game. But, if a player *can* perform some physical activity – limited though he may be – it is important to include him in aspects of the game as quickly as possible, even if it is only for walk-through situations.

This mindset is critical for accelerating the return-to-play process. The players who have the best resiliency are those who understand that health is a continuum, and who avoid thinking "I can't do anything because I'm hurt." It's important that coaches work together with their players to find ways to keep injured players involved with team activities as much as possible.

6.1 Health, Stress, and Performance

Each body system – from the nervous system to the endocrine or musculoskeletal systems – has a limited capacity for handling stress. Stress does not exist in isolation; lifestyle, competing and training all build up stress over time.

It's crucial to acknowledge that the body has a **functional reserve** that cannot be excessively drained. Humans have a limited supply of energy on which to draw for handling stressors, whether they are physical, cognitive, or emotional.

Different circumstances impact how the body allocates this functional reserve. When a player has the flu, for instance, a huge percentage of his overall stress capacity is dedicated to combating the virus. If he can take time off to recover, his body will typically bounce back in a week or so.

But, say a player has the flu and decides to play in a crucial playoff game. Now he's been introduced to another stressor that might exceed the total stress load his body can handle. It's now more likely that he will get injured or his flu will get worse after the game. He may have to battle the illness for two or three weeks, instead of the one week it would have taken to recover had he rested.

Now consider the stress of traveling to away games. A team might decide to do a light practice the day after a hectic travel day and one of the players steps awkwardly during one of the drills. Normally this would not be a big deal and his **proprioception** – his sense of body positioning and movement – would give proper feedback about where his foot is in relation to the ground and he would adjust accordingly. This time, however, travel fatigue has drained his functional reserve so much that he is unable to adjust, and he sprains his ankle.

Both examples show that coaches can't look at performance output in isolation. It's important to continually assess the players' overall functional reserve and identify events and situations that put inordinate stress on one or more systems. Coaches can then scale back the training or practice load as necessary. This will improve the overall health of players and preempt issues like illness, injury, and burnout. Players can also continually be encouraged to take ownership of their own positive recovery habits as best as possible (which, unfortunately, is a difficult challenge).

6.2   Psycho-Physiological Health

Psychological, emotional, and spiritual health are key in determining not only the success of athletic careers, but also the quality of life that players enjoy during and after their playing days. Remember, the body and brain are one.

When it comes to the health of our players, we must see
the body and brain as one.

That said, the most important "psychologist" is always the head coach, simply because the head coach directs the overall vision, culture, and mood of the team. Therefore, the head coach has a great deal of responsibility on his shoulders to steer the psychological ship and lead it into championship waters. But of course, when encountering player issues that are significant, a player needs to be directed to a psychologist or psychiatrist as soon as these issues are recognized.

6.2.1 Health and Longevity

The length of a player's career and the player's longevity after retiring are inseparable. The same habits that a sport team might cultivate to squeeze out every ounce of performance potential while remaining healthy – like getting adequate recovery, dialing in nutrition, and managing stress – also form the core of a long and sustainable lifestyle.

It's a coach's role to weigh certain acts of sacrifice, like having a player play through injury, against the long-term welfare of the players for whom he is responsible. It can be difficult to take the long view when a championship is on the line, but players are people and their life worth far exceeds what they achieve on the field. The organization has a duty to protect players so they can enjoy a long, healthy life.

6.2.2 Training Smarter, Not Harder

In training and practice, components of intensity, volume, and rest should be distributed intelligently. If coaches want to train at a very high intensity, they need to acknowledge that longer recovery periods will be necessary. If wanting to purposely minimize rest periods, then it must be accepted that intensity will have to drop to a sustainable level.

As a summary to help mitigate most training-related health risks, coaches can keep the following in mind:

Don't suddenly increase intensity of workloads.

When training or practicing, design the exercises to allow for gradual, sensible increases in parameters of intensity, volume, density, and collision. This gives players' bodies a chance to adapt as they progress. Each game will be different in terms of movements, problems, and overall chaos, but the fitness-related qualities associated with each game will be similar. While it's impossible to perfectly prepare players, they can be given a better chance of staying healthy and performing at a high level by gradually building up to game-related fitness.

Always emphasize quality execution above all else.

There will be moments when coaches want players to move very fast and powerfully and other moments when they want players to achieve a higher volume of work and challenge endurance. No matter what the emphasis of training or practice might be, if coaches can focus on quality of execution over attaining a pre-determined volume of repetitions, they will know when to add or cut back on the work, as dictated by quality.

Carefully observe players and allow them to rest if needed.

"Carefully" is the operative word here, since it's important to push players beyond discomfort so they can adapt and grow but, while avoiding overtraining them. There's a difference between a player that's simply breathing heavy and a player that is completely exhausted. If a player starts falling over or can't catch his breath, it's worth it to pull him out for a few minutes so he can get some water and breathe deeply before going back to exercising or practicing.

Give high-risk players an extra rest period.

If it is determined that certain players are at risk due to coming back from injury or dealing with sickness, coaches must proceed with caution. Similarly, if a player has a medical risk factor like sickle cell trait or diabetes, coaches need to be aware of how to handle him appropriately in training and practice. If players are truly at risk, then it's worth giving them a little more rest and finding the absolute minimum effective dose for improvement.

6.3   The Player Personality

Coaches can't prepare players to win without first acknowledging their personalities. It's paramount for a coach to understand how to communicate with a player based on an understanding of who that player is and how he operates. But, while many organizations are comfortable measuring objective or biological markers in statistics and sports science, it's often uncomfortable to investigate the "fuzzy" world of evaluating player personalities. However, to get a full picture of player health and find an additional performance edge, the organization owes it to players to take personality assessments seriously - especially when recruiting or drafting players.

6.3.1   Hippocrates, Psychology, and Physiology

Hippocrates was among the first influential thinkers to suggest that the mind and body are one. He believed that there were physiological causes and remedies for psychological problems. As it turns out, he was on to something.

Researchers now know that mood - long thought to be exclusive to the realm of the mind - is largely determined by neurotransmitter and hormone levels in the body. When it comes to the psychology of players, levels of testosterone, estrogen, dopamine, and other chemicals not only govern the physical impact of training loads but also impact how players think and feel. As Stanford psychiatrist and behavioral sciences professor Robert Malenka puts it, "The brain is what mediates our feelings, thoughts, and behaviors."

Another Stanford professor, Dr. Robert Sapolsky, has an entire book about the biology of behavior, appropriately titled *Behave: The Biology of Humans at Our Best and Worst*. In this text, Sapolsky takes a wonderfully-organized approach in describing biological phenomena occurring during different time periods surrounding a behavior: one second before, seconds to minutes before, hours to days before, days to months before and even centuries to millennia before – stressing the undeniable connection between biology, behaviors and culture.

According to Sapolsky, it "actually makes no sense to distinguish between aspects of a behavior that are 'biological' and those that would be described as, say, 'psychological' or 'cultural.' Utterly intertwined."

6.4   The Resilient Player

It's not a stretch to say that most athletes with long, successful careers have proven to be resilient and have sustainable lifestyles. This doesn't necessarily mean that they have completely avoided injury, but rather that the environment they've been in, the habits they've created, and the choices they've made have all contributed positively to their overall health and well-being. Their dedication has fostered a persistence that enables them to bounce back from adversity, while their commitment to their overall well-being has enabled them to stay in the game long enough to leave a legacy.

Plenty of players can blaze a trail at the highest level of sport for a couple of years while partying, abusing alcohol and drugs, and failing to take care of themselves. But rarely do such players continue to play at a high level or keep their personal lives on an even keel for long. Eventually there will be a reckoning - physically, psychologically, emotionally, and/or spiritually. Thus, the key to helping players achieve all they're capable of in sport and in life is helping them be resilient human beings who are part of a sustainable organization.

7 Preparing the Team

Effectively programming for game day requires that coaches expose players to training stimuli in a carefully ordered sequence. Team preparation programming must accommodate the various internal and external biological cycles to which all players are exposed. Their bodies are in a constant state of adaptation, searching for ways to maintain an internal balance - known as **homeostasis** - as best as possible.

This equilibrium is key in understanding the stress response of the body. Coaches must accept and obey the biological laws that govern this process. As a result, the functional state of a player at any given time will dictate what he is able to do on a given day, which will subsequently determine what he is able to do the next day and so on.

Players are in a constant state of adaptation, searching
for ways to maintain homeostasis.

The best-written training program is irrelevant if it doesn't consider the functional starting point of the players. Fatigued players and rested players respond very differently to the same program. So, coaches need to think about the physical, emotional, and cognitive status of players always to plan forthcoming sessions.

The load that players experience playing football games is a crucial factor. If the team has played more games than usual – like having played Sunday and now preparing for a Thursday night game – and the players have dealt with travel stress, then coaches must reduce the team preparation load so that the players' minds and bodies aren't overwhelmed.

7.1 The Programming Elements

We refer to the weekly training cycle as a **morphocycle,** and it is based on the time available between games. We will explain the morphocycle in more detail soon, but for now we can concisely state that it provides a balance among stressors in order to maximize player adaptation and learning.

Broadly speaking, the morphocycle should manage the four main elements of training and practice: volume, intensity, density, and collision. During the week, coaches can manage these elements so that players aren't overstressed, and performance is maximized. For example, some days will be high-volume and low-intensity while other days are low-volume and high-intensity.

7.1.1   Volume

Volume simply refers to how much total work is being done on a training day. Volume can be measured in terms of time, number of repetitions, time under tension, or total distance covered, to name a few examples. In a football practice, coaches and sport science personnel can quantify volume by the total number of repetitions during drills or how much of the field is being covered. They can also total up the number of plays between the unit and team periods in practice to help identify practice volume.

Global positioning systems (GPS) can be valuable for monitoring practice volume as well. The sport science staff can use GPS to measure the distances covered by each player and decide which volume ranges make sense for the team goals. In strength and conditioning, coaches can track volume by total number of sprints, explosive efforts like jump takeoffs, as well as the total number of high-intensity lifts.

7.1.2   Intensity

Intensity is a measure of the magnitude of an output. In strength and conditioning, intensity would refer to how fast a player sprinted, how high a player jumped, or how much weight a player lifted. In football practice, it refers to the speed at which work is done. This requires clarification: an intense practice can occur even if the players are not moving at their actual maximum speeds. The closer a football practice is to a game-like environment - where players are operating at or above game speed - the more intense the practice will be.

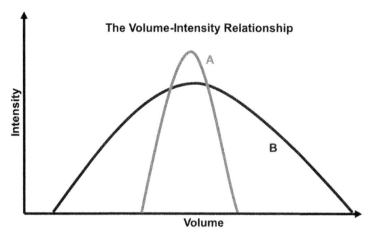

The Volume-Intensity Relationship

The impact of training on the central nervous system is determined by the INTESITY x VOLUME, so above we can see that the impact of curve A is less than the impact of curve B, despite the intensity of curve A being higher.

7.1.3 Density

Density reflects the frequency of work and break periods. In football practice, if coaches want to develop endurance, they can have players run several plays in a limited time frame, which is indicative of high-density. This is because many repetitions will occur with little to no breaks between them.

Conversely, if coaches want to see higher movement speeds from players, they can strategically give them longer breaks between plays so that they are fresher and move faster...a low-density practice. In strength and conditioning, performing exercises in a circuit fashion with minimal rest time is an example of a high-density workout. High-density is associated with minimal rest and low-density is associated with long or complete rest.

7.1.4 Collision

There's no question that football is a high-collision sport by nature. At its essence, collision refers to the vibrational force that players absorb. So, the higher the impact between two bodies, the greater the influence of collision. From this standpoint, one can understand how the catch phase of an Olympic lift is high collision, as are plyometric activities where players must absorb a lot of vibrational force upon ground contact.

Collision is a necessary form of preparation, but it must be managed carefully to avoid overstressing player body structures. In sport science, the staff can gain insight into how much collision the players are experiencing with the use of integrated accelerometry technology. This information, coupled with GPS measurement, may prove highly valuable in determining a valid picture of total stress load from training and practice.

7.2   Working Backwards from the Game

Training sessions that differ in levels of volume, intensity, density and collision will require different time periods for recovery. Each practice will produce distinct stimuli for players' minds and bodies, and these stimuli will cause different physiological responses, depending on the magnitude of their exposure.

7.2.1   Recovery Rates and Training Residuals

It's important to have a basic understanding of how certain training loads will impact player biological functioning. For example, it will take players at least a few days to start recovering, both physically and mentally, from playing a game, and the same is true of a high-collision and high-intensity practice session. It is a coach's responsibility to understand how each day of practice is affecting his players' minds and bodies.

Fatigue is a necessary part of the training process. Fatigue serves as the signal to cells, telling them to synthesize specific proteins needed to restructure the body so it can adapt and grow. But too much fatigue leads to overtraining and under-recovery, a point-of-no-return where players will start shutting down rather than building up.

If coaches have some understanding of how different loads will cause different forms of fatigue, they can strategize and sequence training and practice to account for different recovery timelines for specific forms of training and give players a better chance of positive adaptation.

Recovery After Exposure			
Physical Emphasis	Practice & Training Examples	Training Load Level	Recovery Period
Game Day Execution	Full competition environment. Maximum levels of volume, intensity, density & collision	Extreme	**≥72 hours** Based on game play exposure
Regeneration	Run-through practice situations at low intensity & low volume CNS activation (neural priming), low volume & moderate intensity lifting	Medium (Retentive)	**12-24 hours** Based on volume & recovery protocols
High-Intensity High-Collision	Tackling/Blocking Frequent changes of direction Olympic lifting & eccentric loading	Large (Developmental)	**48-72 hours** Based on volume & recovery protocols
High-Volume High-Density	High number of practice plays (60%+ game volume) w/ minimal rest periods Aerobic, strength endurance & hypertrophy work	Substantial (Developmental)	**24-48 hours** Based on intensity & recovery protocols
High-Speed	Practice speed of decision-making & execution Low volume sprinting, low impact jumps/throws Concentric or explosive lifting – very low or no eccentric loading	Substantial (Developmental)	**24-48 hours** Based on volume & recovery protocols
Restoration	Run-through & review practice situations at low intensity & low volume Active recovery, blood flow enhancement	Small (Restorative)	**≤12 hours** Based on volume & recovery protocols

In addition, different forms of training will result in **training residuals,** which are essentially the after-effects of training stimuli. Training residuals indicate how long the body will stay activated for certain physical qualities after training.

For example, the time frame that a player's body stays activated for endurance after performing endurance work is different than how his body stays activated after explosive activity. Much of the research on training residuals has been reported by Dr. Vladimir Issurin, and we have provided a table on the next page summarizing his findings.

This information, in conjunction with recovery rates, allows coaches to emphasize different loading parameters on different days in a carefully ordered sequence, to respect the biological laws of adaptation. Once coaches know how long the effects of the stimuli might last, they can work backward from the next game when scheduling the morphocycle.

Working backward from the next game provides the ability to program in real time, focusing on what players are doing from session to session. By using the Game Model to help decide the structure of the week, coaches can adapt the Game Plan and the strength and conditioning coaches can always design sessions to suit the current state of the players.

Work backwards to move forward.

Residual Effects After Exposure		
Following Period of Development		
Performance Quality	**Duration of Residual**	**Physiological Adaptations**
Anaerobic Power & Capacity	**14-22 Days**	Increased anaerobic enzymes (2-20%), high acidosis buffering capacity, increased glycogen storage, higher lactate utilization
Aerobic Power & Capacity	**25-35 Days**	Increased aerobic enzymes (40-90%), increased number of mitochondria, increased capillary density, greater oxygen transport, increased glycogen storage, higher rate of fat metabolism
Speed & Power	**2-8 Days**	Improved neuromuscular interactions, improved motor control, increased phosphocreatine storage (2-5%)
Maximum Strength	**25-35 Days**	Greater activation of muscle fibers (motor units), improved motor unit synchronization, increased firing rate of motor unit signaling, increased muscle fiber size (hypertrophy)
Strength Endurance	**10-20 Days**	Increased size of slow-twitch muscle fibers, increased anaerobic & aerobic enzymes, improved local blood circulation, improved tolerance to acidic build-up

Another reason to work backward from the game is because the game itself is the only measuring stick for team performance. The players *must* be ready for game day, both physically and mentally. If they are not, then the organization has failed to account for what's most important - *the game*!

A sport game is inherently complex, and the events of the game occur in a nonlinear manner. To be effective, training and practice should mirror this complexity and nonlinearity. By structuring practices in a multi-faceted way – considering tactical, technical, physical and psychological factors – coaches can simplify player education by breaking things down into parts. In this way, players can develop perception-action skills in practice more effectively than in some traditional systems that tend to isolate physical actions.

> *We work backwards because the game itself is the only*
> *measuring stick for performance.*

Using the game as a guide for training, there's no disconnect between what happens in the practice facility and what players are to achieve during the game. By keeping everything intact, players can develop positive playing habits through experiences representing what they will encounter in the next game. The key principles are introduced, encouraged, and reinforced during team practice, so that players develop habits that are conducive to the Game Plan and its objectives. This way, when it comes time to react to a game-time situation, the automatic response will be positive.

Learning experiences created for players can be devised and executed within the context of the Game Moments and their associated Micro Moments. Every exercise or drill conducted in practice is relevant to how the head coach wants his players to play during the game.

7.3   Strategies for Learning Skills

The most important distinguishing factor for a football player is positional skill. This means that all forms of strength and conditioning, practice design, volume, and everything else must lead to players operating efficiently and effectively in practice and on game day. To develop skill, coaches need to manage volume, intensity, density, and collision appropriately to improve the learning opportunity and outcome.

7.3.1   Volume and Quantity of Work

Whether trying to teach a player how to properly squat in the weight room, perform a linear sprint, or develop his perception-action cycle through carefully designed drills in practice, it's necessary to keep volume lower when training a new skill in order to maximize learning.

This is a big reason why we believe the use of run-throughs in individual periods of practice are invaluable. These run-throughs can take players through the perception-action cycle in very controlled, low-intensity settings. Coaches are teaching them which keys to read and the appropriate responses, based upon their positional alignment, assignment and technique.

A high volume or high number of reps – a "more is better" approach – will undermine the positive impact of most learning experiences. Volume should be increased only after the player demonstrates the ability to perform the skill with intensity and density.

7.3.2   Intensity and Quality of Training

Learning new skills is a high-intensity activity for the brain, so quality is prioritized above all else. Once a player can do something well a few times, coaches can have him perform more repetitions to show that he can perform the skill while dealing with acute fatigue.

Players must be constantly reminded that skills take time to develop and a few repetitions with great focus will go much further for their development than a bunch of repetitions where focus is absent.

7.3.3   Density and Frequency of Training

Density needs to be low when introducing a new skill. In football, breaks are part of the game – the players move, the whistle blows, and there is a break before they move again. Not to mention, every play, every movement, and every second will be different from the last. It's worthwhile to replicate this in practice.

It's better for players to focus intently for a few minutes and then take a break so they can replay what they've just learned in their minds. Coaches can give players the opportunity to figure it out, and this principle carries over to learning new exercises in the weight room as well. A player is not likely going to be great at squatting, lunging, power cleaning, or any other exercise until put in positions to understand these exercises and how to efficiently execute them.

7.3.4   Collision Considerations

Collision is obviously more exaggerated in some activities than others. Football is a contact sport involving bodily impact between players. When a cornerback puts a big hit on a wide receiver, both players' bodies are subjected to a high vibrational load due to the violent, explosive force of the cornerback projecting into the wide receiver.

Such an impact is multi-directional and off axis, increasing the demand on each player's bodies to dissipate the forces being generated. This demand for the players' structures to dissipate forces is a primary reason why structural resiliency (building connective tissue integrity) is paramount, including strengthening players' necks to reduce concussive blows to the head.

Even activities like sprinting involve repeated impact of the runners' feet into the ground, generating a large amount of ground reaction force per step – upwards of over five times body weight in high-level sprinters as reported by Dr. Ken Clark. These ground impacts take their toll on muscles, bones, ligaments, and tendons. This type of collision becomes more intense with harder the ground surfaces like practicing on a cold, icy field.

While it's not necessary for a team sport player to perform the same volume of sprinting or plyometrics as track and field athletes, these sessions must still be accounted for in order to understand how the literal impact of these drills might affect everything else in the weekly cycle.

7.4   Preparing the Team to Win Games

The goal for any team is simple: win the next game. Form follows function. Having the biggest, fastest, and strongest players in the country but no wins to show for it signifies a lack of effectiveness. All aims of preparation are secondary to the primary aim of the team – win games.

It's easy to get caught up in the means of how a team prepares – how they practice, what exercises they do in the weight room, and so on. But this is a backwards approach. Designs for practice and for the weight room should reflect the exact principles and style of play that the head coach expects to see on game day.

If coaches take and borrow means and methods from another coach who has an entirely different approach to the Game Model, then how much good is it doing? The end dictates the means. In other words, how a head coach wants his team to play the game will determine every form of preparation.

> *What we design for practice and for the weight room*
> *should both be based on the same exact principles.*

Preparation should focus on providing players with contextualized, guided experiences that result in the acquisition of what the playbook demands, including how to use effective skills and enhancing tactical awareness. It's a team's responsibility to point the way for players, and it's the job of players to be fully engaged in learning.

7.4.1   *The Morphocycle – Maximizing Each Training Week*

The term *morphocycle* refers to the structure and format of a preparation cycle. The preparation (or training) cycle is the flexible period between two games. The morphocycle refers to the sessions of training and experiences to which the players are exposed during that period.

The root *morpho* can be easily understood as "structure and form," implying that the training week has a definitive and carefully designed structure.

The morphocycle is not part of a periodization approach, nor is it an isolated physical preparation method. Rather, it is a balance of different training elements that make up the weekly training cycle. Instead of thinking broadly over large ranges of time, the morphocycle focuses on one week at a time. Everything depends on where players are currently in terms of health and the four coactives, as well as where they need to be by game day.

Within each morphocycle, there should be a balance of learning experiences stressing different amounts of volume, intensity, density, and collision. There should also be a balance of technical, tactical, physical, and psychological stressors to help ensure that players have enough work in each area to prompt positive adaptation, but not so much that they can't recover properly before the next game.

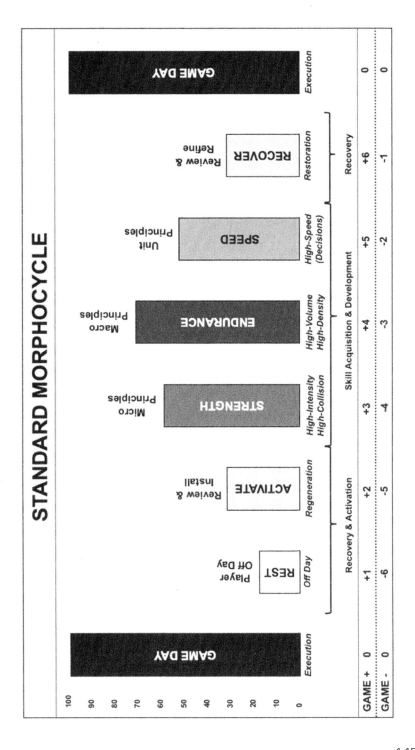

STANDARD MORPHOCYCLE

	REST	ACTIVATE	STRENGTH	ENDURANCE	SPEED	RECOVER	GAME DAY
	Player Off Day	Review & Install	Micro Principles	Macro Principles	Unit Principles	Review & Refine	
	Off Day	Regeneration	High-Intensity High-Collision	High-Volume High-Density	High-Speed (Decisions)	Restoration	Execution
		Recovery & Activation		Skill Acquisition & Development		Recovery	
GAME +	+1	+2	+3	+4	+5	+6	0
GAME -	-6	-5	-4	-3	-2	-1	0

100
90
80
70
60
50
40
30
20
10
0

Within the morphocycle, the Four-Coactive Model must fit harmoniously. Essentially, there will be four different coactive pathways throughout the weekly cycle, and players will fluctuate in terms of their tactical, technical, physical, and psychological readiness. The purpose of monitoring training is for the four coactives to function to the highest degree possible heading into the next game.

7.4.2.1   The Three Phases of Team Preparation

The three phases below can broadly help formulate a plan to prepare a team between games. When there's less time available because of a short week, phase two can be minimized or skipped:

1. Individual correction and recovery from the previous game.
2. Acquisition of learning experiences that improve tactics and further the Game Plan objectives.
3. Rehearsal of patterns before facing the next opponent.

These phases should be adaptable and responsive to the actual schedule from week to week. The reality is that there are no ideal situations in sport, so it's important to work as effectively as possible in any given scenario.

Players are tasked with understanding why they were or were not effective in specific Game Moments. The key here is to focus on solutions, not stress over the problems. Players are not idiots, and when they mess up an assignment or lack the execution they hoped for, they are usually aware of it. This is especially true when using a sound Game Model.

> *The key is to focus on solutions, not stress over the problems.*

7.4.2.2   Communicating with Principles

The solutions communicated directly to players should almost always be in the form of principles, not directions. If a linebacker takes a risk and goes for the quarterback, giving up his coverage zone, then coaches can reiterate to him the Micro Principles of Defensive Play, such as defensive support, cover, and compactness so he realizes how he put his team at risk by directly going against these principles.

In addition, coaches can strategically use the practices earlier in the week to expose individual players to learning environments that allow them to work on maximizing their dominant qualities and mitigating the limitations to their performance. Performance-limiting factors could be related to tactical issues like poor player decisions, or technical issues like an offensive lineman struggling to drive his opponent off the ball in rushing situations.

It's important that the work done during positional and unit periods is not done in isolation or in an abstract setting, but in a manner that's like the game itself. To give an example, if a lineman is struggling to drive his opponent off the ball, having him drive-block a sled will likely not help his ability to perform in the game. The sled will not hit him back or try to evade his block. Instead, positional drills where he must block another human player (like he would in the game) will have far more direct transfer from a technical standpoint. Every experience that players have in practice should accurately represent some facet of the game itself.

In addition to improving individual learning experiences, practice environments should impact group and team dynamics in a positive manner. Having one stellar defensive end is not enough to win a championship; the entire defensive line must understand how to operate efficiently and effectively.

"There are so many different variations [of plays]...but if our kids understand concepts, we really only have to teach it once to them and then...even in the middle of a game we could even scheme it up...something that we see against the defense...maybe we've never run it before, but [our players] know that it's...one of the premier concepts that we have in our offense."

- Rob Weiner, Plant High School, Tampa (FL)

7.4.3   Tactical Considerations

Here the concern is with the development of strategy, which is based on achieving certain objectives within the Game Moments as part of the Game Plan. Tactical considerations are based upon the upcoming opponent and should be designed to maximize the strengths of the team and exploit the opposition's known weaknesses.

When designing tactics, with every play called, every formation used, every player action, and so on must exist a defined context and purpose. At many levels of football, but especially the lower levels like high school, coaches might be tempted to copy the tactics of another team that has had success, assuming they can also find the same success. The problem with this approach is that they are forgetting *why* that successful team used those tactics in the first place.

Focus on reasons.

Ask Why, Why, Why

Tactics must be purposeful and based on the talents of the available personnel. The high school coach that tries to run a Power-I formation and play smash-mouth football with an offensive line averaging 175 lbs. is not going to find much success. It's best to first understand the team and its abilities, then determine the tactics.

7.4.4   Technical Considerations

Although coaches might have a desired outcome in mind for a certain player, they can help him solidify the relationship between his technical and tactical coactives by allowing him to select what he believes is the right skill for the situation based on his previous experience and the experiences provided for him in practice.

Unfortunately, many coaches have become obsessive over "perfect" form – whether it's throwing a perfect spiral or having an exact foot placement coming out of a backpedal – without teaching players to self-regulate and critically learn. There is no such thing as perfect form, only perfect principles.

There is no such thing as perfect form, only perfect
principles.

It is much more efficient to focus on the job itself and set up scenarios for players to make decisions and execute habits on their own initiative, with whatever form they choose to get the job done. For elite players, technical ability is both self-correcting and constantly developing. Skill execution has inherent variability and will change depending on the infinite number of possibilities that each game presents.

Does this mean coaches should not coach at all? Of course not! If coaches spot a player moving in an unsafe manner according to biomechanical principles, then they should certainly intervene and mitigate it before acute or chronic injury ensues. However, the primary role is to serve as a guide and teacher. Put the focus of communication on explaining the situation, not giving absolute directions on how to solve it, although hints can be provided when players are struggling to be effective.

7.4.4.1   The Test of Writing Your Name

The way a player moves will change depending on the current context. Remember, it's impossible to replicate the exact same motion twice. Don't believe us? Here's a small test first explained to us by our friend Shawn Myszka.

Get a piece of paper and a pen and write your name on it as quickly as you can. This is an activity that you've done your entire life since learning how to write. Now, try and write it again at the same speed, in the same way. Are the lines different this time? Of course! But were you any less *effective* at successfully writing your name? Of course not! Though it wasn't written exactly the same, you still managed to successfully write your name both times.

If it's impossible to take a simple, largely rehearsed pattern like writing your name and replicate the exact same motion twice, then how can coaches expect players to do so in the complex, chaotic nature of a football game?

Can you imagine trying to teach a high school student how to drive while constantly staying next to him in the car, giving him an entire play-by-play of what to do and when? He would never be able to drive without you there. Instead, it's better that he knows the traffic laws, what different street signs mean, when to use turn indicators, and so on. With these principles in place, he can figure out how best to drive the vehicle while obeying the rules.

149

*Create experiences that encourage outcomes and allow
players to decide how to achieve them.*

7.4.4.2   Resiliency Over Robustness

Players are better served if coaches concentrate on creating experiences that encourage certain outcomes but leave it up to the players to decide how to achieve them. Repetition of certain drills can help players make autonomous choices during competition, but variations within exercises will help facilitate continued learning and skill improvement which can be applied when it counts.

When things go unexpectedly, players then have the requisite fortitude to improvise and have a better chance of making something positive happen. This is the difference between having robust players and resilient players.

Repetitive drills can help players become more robust in specific situations, but the players will not be able to cope with chaos when things go awry. In contrast, players who are resilient will not only be hard to break, but they will almost always find a way to bounce back.

7.4.4.3   Skill Specificity

As players amass more game experiences, they will refine and improve performance of certain skills and will be able to apply them effectively in a broader range of situations – they will become more resilient. If players are encouraged to explore and find solutions to sport problems, they will typically find the expression of a skill that best suits them and the situations in which they find themselves.

The best players can select the appropriate skill and execute it so quickly and effectively that their opponents cannot prevent the intended result – like intercepting a pass or setting up a pass rush without being touched. This decision is not a result of moving for the sake of moving but exists in a tactical context that changes based on factors like the player's proximity to the ball, teammates, opponents, end zone, as well as the remaining time in the game.

Technical execution depends on physical and psychological factors. If a player doesn't believe he is good enough to execute a certain motion, then he likely won't.

Coaches can work with players on finding the skill set that best emphasizes their individuality and what they are able to bring to the table.

7.4.4.4   Adding Perception

Players need to add perception to their training to make their skill sets more applicable to an actual game. This doesn't always require eleven-on-eleven team situations, but skill training should encompass perception as much as possible to help dictate which movements should be used and why.

In his book *Gamespeed,* author Ian Jeffreys does a wonderful job of illustrating the target context for common sports movements. He explains how different movements found across team sports will serve similar purposes - what he refers to as target functions.

For example, for a defensive back, the target function of a backpedal is to read his keys while simultaneously staying in an athletic position and preparing to react and move to where his keys are telling him to go. Simply backpedaling for the sake of backpedaling is not keeping true to context.

The same concept applies to a shuffle for a linebacker. If coaches encourage him to shuffle as fast as possible, there is limited context. In the game, if the linebacker must get somewhere immediately, he will just turn and run while maintaining leverage. The shuffle is simply a transitional motion used for reading the field.

"I have never seen somebody in a football game run behind 10 bags and then go and tackle somebody."

- Mike Ricci, Garnet Valley High School, Glen Mills (PA)

7.4.5   Techno-Tactical Preparation

Tactical and technical actions cannot be separated. As such, coaches and scouts are tasked with evaluating and developing technical skill execution within the tactical framework of the Game Plan. This synthesis can be understood as **techno-tactical preparation.**

Consider an NFL quarterback who must go through an incredibly involved sequence of decisions and actions - with precision - while a rush of giant men is coming to tackle him and tens of thousands of people in the stands are yelling and screaming. Quarterbacks need competence for skill selection and execution abiding by the framework of the Game Plan and enough psychological fortitude to handle the emotional pressure of the moment. Moreover, they must consider how the other 10 members of the offense are operating in conjunction with what they are seeing.

It's not enough for players to possess high-level technical skills in isolation; they also need to express these skills as part of real-time solutions to challenges and problems that arise during every game. The ability to match a skill to an issue and apply it at just the right time is often what elevates players to the elite echelon.

This is possible only when they're able to combine previous experiences with a quick, accurate assessment of current game conditions and select and apply the right technical movement at the right moment. When looking at the layers of complexity, it's truly amazing that any player is ever able to execute effectively and consistently.

7.4.6   Psychological Considerations

Player psychological states are a direct result of influences on and off the field. It's not uncommon for players to bring their off-field mental stresses into the team atmosphere, so coaches must always be mindful of changes to player behaviors.

They must dedicate themselves to learning about all their players as people, not as roster spots that are used like pieces of a board game. During the season, coaches can have multiple conversations with players and be attentive, so they learn about their emotional and cognitive states and their sense of belonging.

7.4.6.1   Emotional Considerations

Emotions govern the way players express themselves in words and deeds. They are also responsible for mood and how well players relate to teammates, coaches, and other members of the organization. Emotions are an expression of a player's personality.

As a rule, the emotional load on the team should be kept as low as possible during the week. The game exerts such a large emotional load on players that they need the intensity to be dialed down during the practice week. The only exception is if a player has checked out and his level of excitation, alertness, or arousal is too low.

In this case, coaches can first converse with the player and try to determine if the issue is related to depression or another emotional issue. But, if they determine that the player is not dealing with any negative emotions, and is instead acting with entitlement or recklessness, they might want to up the emotional ante by introducing a real or imagined threat. By "threat" we certainly don't mean anything harmful, but actions like reducing playing time or dropping the player lower on the depth chart.

Good coaches keep the emotional load low by ensuring that there is emotional control in every practice session. Part of building resilient players is getting them comfortable being uncomfortable, which really refers to challenging the brain more than the body.

When players become accustomed to dealing with chaos and unexpected game situations in practice, they will learn to adapt by reducing their emotional discomfort when things don't go as planned.

7.4.6.2 Cognitive Considerations

Cognition involves how players learn. It's the area responsible for grasping the strategies and tactical concepts of the playbook. When progressing through the complexity of the playbook, it is important for coaches to be mindful of cognitive load since players need to be mentally fresh come game day.

Most of the learning load should be concentrated in the first few days of the morphocycle, at least in terms of conscious learning. Later in the week, focus can shift toward more subconscious experiential learning. Cognitive loading occurs off the field as well with classes, team meetings and film study, so the volume of time spent in meetings should be managed carefully.

If a player becomes emotionally unbalanced or has a spiritual issue (discussed next), cognitive learning often suffers, and the quality of preparation will decline. Similarly, if the cognitive load is too great, a player can suffer psychologically. Emotion, cognition, and spirituality are intertwined and cannot be separated from each other.

7.4.6.3   Spiritual Considerations

With spirituality, we are really referring to how a player views himself in relation to his team and the outside world. Spirituality plays into the desire to "be a part of something bigger." It concerns self-focused questions like, "who am I?", "what am I doing here?", and "why is football meaningful to me?" as well as outward-facing considerations like the importance of teammates and coaches.

The key to spirituality is for the team to show a sense of unity, culture or spirit during practice, workouts, and games. The basis of anyone's psychological perspective is their belief system. This is the player's fundamental and conscious understanding of the world. This can be based on the player's faith and religious affiliations, but also results from the mentors he has had, the influence of his family, life experiences, education, and his societal culture. All these factors cross-pollinate and influence each other in the spiritual dimension of the psychological coactive.

From a team perspective, it's important that players feel a sense of unity. The team is a family, and the players will be part of its culture. They will be exposed to the team environment at the team facilities every day; from the locker room, to the practice fields, to the weight room, to the dining halls, and in classes and social events. In addition, all players will be part of a family of relatives, a friendship circle and a wider community that branches beyond football. All these different settings will impact each player and his state of mind, for good or ill.

For these reasons, it's necessary that coaches maintain a constant state of involvement in the spiritual state of the team. This should stay consistent throughout the weekly cycle and will require continual effort, since players are subject to exterior forces like relationships with family and friends.

7.4.6.4   What About Mental Toughness?

Cultivating mental strength is every bit as important as developing physical strength. The key to sustained "mental toughness" lies within six areas: focus, self-efficacy, frustration tolerance, self-confidence, determination, and persistence. These traits should be encouraged every day during team preparation. Psychological resilience should become a cultural value that every member of the squad recognizes and embraces.

However, mental toughness is *not* a result of putting players through military drills or other physically excruciating activities. As with everything else, mental toughness is situational and context dependent. People will only show mental toughness in the activities they have learned to conquer.

If coaches expect the team to show mental toughness during a football game, then they need to expose players to tough game situations, not have them collectively carry logs for miles or wade into freezing water. Having worked with elite special forces operators, Fergus can assure you that they shake their heads in dismay when they see videos of these activities in team sports.

Mental toughness is specific to the task at hand.

While military team-building exercises might serve as nice experiences to prove that a team can conquer something together, there's not much it will do for them when they're losing in the fourth quarter and need to score as soon as possible. In football, mental toughness is specific to the task at hand and must be fostered with game experiences and game-like preparation exercises.

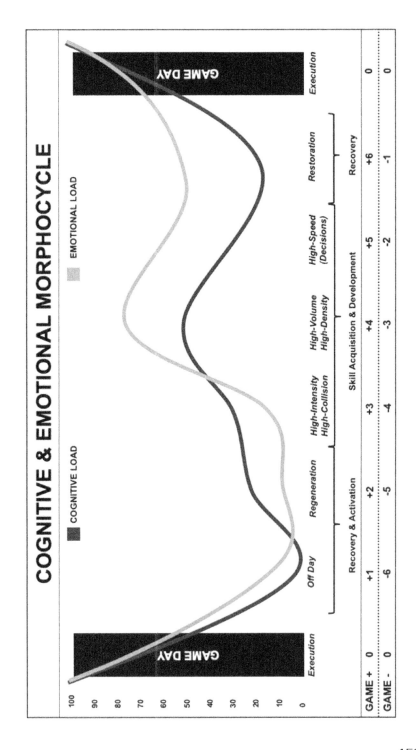

COGNITIVE & EMOTIONAL MORPHOCYCLE

156

7.4.7   Physical Considerations

For players to implement the tactical and technical elements of the Game Plan on game day, coaches must help them physically prepare to do so. This is where a strength and conditioning staff that understands the Game Model and the associated Game Plan is invaluable.

Understanding how the physical stress of the practice week interplays with the tactical, technical, and psychological coactives can help the strength staff understand when a given amount of physical training is enough to build players up, but not break them down.

Coaches can program each morphocycle using an approach based on the **minimum-effective-dose**. The aim of this approach is to place just enough stress on players' bodies during practice and in the weight room to produce positive adaptations while ensuring they are ready to apply their physical outputs at their fullest potential on game day.

Looking at strength and conditioning through a skill-centric mindset prevents thinking only in terms of the muscles involved. Instead, strength and conditioning exercises each have their own miniature technical, tactical, and psychological components.

Observe strength and conditioning through a skill-centric mindset.

7.4.7.1   Weight Room Skill

When seeing improvements in how much a player squats, how high he jumps, or how fast he runs, what is really on display is improvement in skill. Players will experience nervous system adaptations such as a rise in technical mastery first, then physical adaptations, like muscle hypertrophy, occur later. The body adapts and changes its physical make-up to support the demands imposed upon it – commonly referred to as the SAID principle (specific adaptations to imposed demands).

When a player runs a faster 40-yard dash, he got better at the skill of sprinting. When he benches more weight, it's because he becomes a better bench-presser.

157

Adaptation takes place *after* performing the skill, not during it, which is why the morphocycle should consider the various recovery rates of different body systems, as well as the sequencing of the training stimuli.

8 Designing the Morphocycle

Players need more than physical and technical development. Coaches must focus on their cognitive characteristics as well. In traditional periodization schemes, the weekly cycles vary training loads to accommodate physical characteristics, but often completely ignore the impact of tactical and psychological stress. This is a very incomplete model. All coactives must be considered when preparing the team for game day.

Therefore, it is suggested to combine the Four-Coactive Model into a single, unified weekly cycle. It should consider the tactical, technical, psychological and physical impact of every team preparation activity, and balance them as best as possible.

This way, on each day, some body systems will be stimulated while others are de-emphasized to promote recovery. The goal is to develop all four coactives simultaneously throughout the year with one goal in mind: getting incrementally better from game-to-game and forming a curve of progression that is sustained throughout the season.

On each day, some body systems are stimulated while others are de-emphasized to promote recovery.

Using the Four-Coactive Model to guide the morphocycle design, the tactical preparation assumes the lead role. Since the tactical preparation is reflective of the Game Model and Game Plan, all training sessions must work backward from what the players are to achieve in the game. The desired tactics will influence the technical skill required, which will be determined by the player's ability to physically perform that skill...all of which will depend on the player's psychological state.

8.1 Balancing Elements of the Morphocycle

One way to manage the daily loading is to stress a different emphasis on each day based on intensity, collision, density and volume:

High-Intensity, High-Collision Practice

These sessions aim to emphasize the central nervous system (CNS) and the structural-anatomical system (muscles, soft tissues, fascia, and bones). Practices will be higher in collision, using short-field situations where more change of direction and contact naturally occur, placing more tension on the body structures from absorbing force.

Examples of high-intensity, high-collision practice situations include short yardage, goal line, field goal, punt block and inside run. Other practice drills include block destruction and tackling circuits.

Examples of high-intensity, high-collision strength and conditioning exercises with muscular tension include catching an Olympic lift, performing plyometrics, or heavy strength training.

High-Volume, High-Density Practice

These sessions aim to emphasize the metabolic system (heart, lungs, and blood flow) to provide energy for continued physical activity. Practices will be higher in volume and density and rest is minimal.

Examples of practice situations include up-tempo, two-minute, and using longer-stretching plays in team periods like deep play-action passes. The common idea is to get vertically down the field and do so with a fast tempo.

Examples of strength and conditioning strategies include general aerobic work, hypertrophy training, or strength endurance circuits where density is high, but overload is minimal.

High-Speed Practice

These sessions aim to emphasize the nervous system in terms of speed of movement and decision-making. Practices will be higher in intensity but with reduced volume and density, along with no collision in terms of tackling or aggressive blocking. The focus will be on exposing players to different situations and challenging the speed of their decision-making.

Examples for practice can include any game situation but with long rest intervals between series while strictly emphasizing execution. This practice is usually performed with helmets only and closer to game day.

Examples of strength and conditioning strategies will include exercises that are explosive, but avoid excessive muscular tension, such as Olympic lifting without the catch phase, box jumps, and strength exercises where players do not have to absorb a lot of force, like performing deadlifts and dropping the bar at the top.

Each day features differing amounts of volume, intensity, density, and collision. No day should rank as "high" for more than two of these four elements, or the players will be physically, cognitively, and emotionally overloaded and will not adapt positively to the stimuli to which they're subjected. For example, it wouldn't be wise to feature high volume, high intensity, and high collision all in one day. One or two days like this could jeopardize the entire morphocycle.

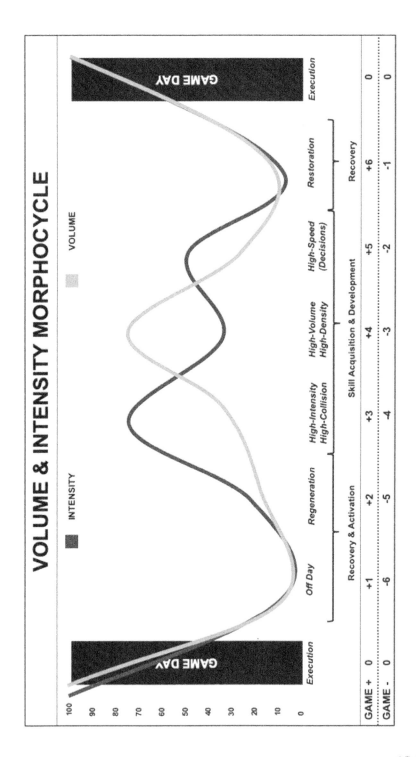

VOLUME & INTENSITY MORPHOCYCLE

8.1.1   Determining & Managing Game Volume

Football has changed over the years. In college football, the number of total offensive plays has risen from around sixty up to eighty plays per game. In the past, it was commonplace for most teams to huddle and take a lot of time away from the 40-second play clock, but now most teams are operating at faster tempos, often snapping the ball every twenty-five to thirty seconds.

Some college teams that really go up-tempo start snapping the ball consecutively every ten to fifteen seconds! Players are becoming leaner and faster as a result of the spread offensive schemes. As the game changes, the game volume changes, and if players expect to optimally prepare, they must adapt with it.

The game can be used as a guide to determine how much work should be done in training and in practice. It's important to state that there are no definitive numbers; there is no "one-size-fits-all" approach to determining practice volume.

The volume will reflect what a team does in terms of the Game Plan, and the training volume will fluctuate naturally to counter what the opponents will do each week. However, there are certain ranges that reflect the functional minimums for which every team must prepare to keep up with the evolution of the game.

8.1.2   The Practice Volume Problem

The problem, as it exists right now, is that most practices are designed strictly based on time. Most days are based upon fitting the most work possible into every designated practice period. Based on alternating volume, intensity, density, and collision, one can understand that there is little rhyme or reason to this approach. With it, it will be difficult to maintain much consistency throughout the week. Recall that consistency is necessary to build desirable habits in players and to prime their bodies with a routine.

The morphocycle is used to help account for everything, especially how each day is going to physically impact players. Adaptation to training is a complex phenomenon that may never be fully understood. But if a framework is provided for the week based on known biological laws, there's a much better chance of achieving readiness come game day.

Coaches can easily manipulate intensity, density, and collision based on the design of the practice activities. The drills themselves will take care of those programming elements. But volume must be carefully considered so that coaches plan an outline of the total stress load spread across the week leading into the game.

Before this can be done, one must account for the volume and demands of the game itself. Once the game demands are understood, morphocycles can be designed with specific volume ranges in mind on specific days. In Level II of this series, we will present some research that has been published on quantifying the physical demands of football to serve as a blueprint for organizing volume.

8.1.3   Game Volume is Team Specific

An important point is that game volume will always be based on a team's offensive scheme. If a coach likes to go up-tempo for most of the game, it's likely he will run more plays than a team that operates at a slower tempo.

Likewise, defenses must prepare to cope with the volume of the opposing offense. No one can predict exactly how many plays will be run, but it's worth calculating and estimated game load so that coaches can formulate a plan that structures the practice loads appropriately throughout the week.

8.1.4   Competition Modeling

To understand how to design practice activities so that they represent the game in realistic settings, while simultaneously respecting the laws of biology, it's important to observe qualitative and quantitative realities of the game. These markers help one understand the performance minimums for which players must prepare. Mapping out this information has been called *competition modeling* and this process can apply to all sports.

A paper by Rhea, Hunter, & Hunter (2006) looked at the qualitative and quantitative data markers of football games at the high school, collegiate, and professional levels in attempts to present a competition model for reference in designing football conditioning programs.

This paper did a wonderful job of presenting the reader with ranges of objective information for average metrics like number of plays per offensive drive, number of offensive series per game, play time durations, and recovery times between plays. The authors even included the number of stoppages - that is, how often the game action was stopped for situations like penalties, time outs, first down measurements, and injuries.

The biggest drawback to this paper is that it was published 13 years ago, and the game has continued to evolve since its publication. Fortunately, there is plenty of data available to help quantify aspects of the game as it stands today. The tables on the next page summarize the findings of the paper by Rhea et. al (2006) along with updated metrics based on how the game is currently being played.

Regardless of whether playing high school, college, or NFL football, these ranges will serve as game minimums for which players should be prepared. Keep in mind that these numbers are just estimated ranges based on our own brief review from multiple resources, including data collected from Fergus' work in college football. A more thorough research review is required to obtain a current, valid competition model. [xxii]

Football Offensive Series Characteristics	
Offensive Series per Game	10-12 Series
Plays per Offensive Series	4-8 Plays
Time of Possession per Series	2-3 Minutes
Total Time of Possession per Game	25-35 Minutes

Football Play Duration Characteristics	
Duration of Play - Run/ Pass	3-6 Seconds
Duration of Play - Punt/ Kickoff (No Touchback)	6-12 Seconds
Time Between Plays (No Stoppages)	20-35 Seconds
Time After Stoppage*	1-3 Minutes
Stoppages per Offensive Drive	0-3 Stoppages

*The time after the end of a quarter or half will be longer than a typical stoppage and will vary considerably between high school, college, and NFL due to factors like television time-outs. Regardless, a complete recovery interval will be characteristic of these stoppages.

Football Snap Count Characteristics for Major Contributing Players	
Player Positional Snaps per Game*	50-80 Snaps
Player Special Team Snaps per Game*	15-25 Snaps

*Based on a range of the most active NFL players during the 2018 regular season (FootballOutsiders.com, LineUps.com)

8.1.5   The Total Stress Load

Each day of the week will pose different degrees of stress on players based on the magnitude of volume, intensity, density, and collision. Coaches can view the week in its entirety and aim to create only enough stimulation in each area to trigger the desired adaptation while empowering each player's body and brain to recover sufficiently so that he can perform his best in the next game. The plan is vital to keeping the balance of the cumulative load manageable.

To be safe, the practice and training loads should always be lower than that of any game. A good rule of thumb is that practice loads should never exceed 75 percent of game-day demands for starting players. As an example, if an offense typically runs 60-70 total plays in a game, then the highest desired practice volume between unit and team periods might be 40-50 repetitions at game-like intensity. A high-volume day like this would only be performed one day during the week and far enough from the game to ensure recovery.

By responsibly and thoughtfully juggling each weekly programming component across the weekly cycle, coaches can optimize the learning experiences they create for players and maximize the adaptation to each stimulus. The game then becomes a qualitative assessment of these learning experiences and a gauge for how effective the preparation was in the preceding morphocycle. It will also serve as an opportunity for coaches to look at which areas need improvement. These assessments directly reflect the Game Model.

The game is the most qualitative assessment of weekly preparation effectiveness.

Football Practice Morphocycle Guide

	Day 1	Day 2	Day 3	Day 4	Day 5	Day 6	Day 7
Tactical Emphasis	Off Day	Review & Install	Micro Principles	Macro Principles	Unit Principles	Review & Refinement	
Physical Emphasis	Rest & Recovery	Activation & Regeneration	High-Intensity High-Collision	High-Volume High-Density	High-Speed	Recovery & Restoration	
Game-Relative Load	Off	30-35%	40-55%	55-70%	35-40%	20-25%	
Practice Physical Goal	Self-assessment of previous game	Nervous system activation; low volume; clean & correct errors from past game; focus on criticizing errors not athletes	High-collision exposure; short yard & tackling; acceleration, deceleration, frequent change of direction	Game endurance; vertically oriented plays downfield; longer distances covered; up-tempo & fast ball speed	Fast movement speed & crisp decision-making; execution should be as smooth as possible with minimal errors	Final run/walk through before the game; refine technique & review various situations	
Group Emphasis	None	Individual Team	Individual Unit	Unit Team	Team	Team	
Sample Situational Emphasis	None	Review run-through of previous game focusing on primary areas of concern going forward.	Greater focus on individual & unit periods – tackling, blocking, & blitzing drills & games. Run-heavy day to emphasize collision.	Shift focus to unit & team periods – rising complexity of player interaction. Pass-heavy day to emphasize endurance.	Focus almost exclusively on team periods, putting all previous work together to cover various situations.	Review & refine all situations covered in previous practices. Emphasize areas of tactical concern.	
Size of Field Space	None	Reduced Spaces	Short & Wide Spaces	Full Field	Reduced Spaces	Reduced Spaces	
Sample Plays per Practice Series	None	3-4 Plays/Series	3-4 Plays/Series	4-8 Plays/Series	3-4 Plays/Series	3-4 Plays/Series	
Sample Density of Series	None	1 Play/Min	1-2 Plays/Min	2-3 Plays/Min	1-2 Plays/Min	1 Play/Min	
Sample	Active Recovery	CNS Activation	High Force	Endurance & Capacity	High Velocity	Active Recovery	
Complimentary Physical Preparation	Soft Tissue & Mobility Work	Low Volume Speed & Power	Acceleration & Strength-Speed	Extensive Aerobic Work	Speed & Speed-Strength	Soft Tissue & Mobility Work	
	Personal Recovery Strategies	Upper Body Strength	Lower Body Strength	Strength Endurance	Lower Body Strength	Personal Recovery Strategies	

GAME DAY (Day 7)

8.2 Volume Exposure

High-volume work is typically performed at a lower intensity and higher density since frequent breaks are not as necessary with the lowered intensity. High-volume days should also be low on the collision scale. When coaches focus on attacking the length of the field, players' muscles are under tension for longer durations, but the eccentric load is reduced since players will move in more linear paths and won't change direction as frequently.

The opposite effect occurs on days that attack the width of the field, where more changes of direction result in more stress on players' hips, knees, and ankles. Every time players change direction, their muscles, tendons, bones and other connective tissues absorb a lot of force before transferring it into positive movement. So, on the high-intensity, high-collision day it's smart to keep volume in moderation so the players aren't overstressed.

It's logical for the high-volume, high-density practice session to feature a lot of "north-south" type of plays and up-tempo situations like hurry-up or two-minute. Passing situations will dominate the session, unless facing a team like Army or Navy where passing plays are rare. It's best not to use goal line or very short-yardage situations for this session and instead capitalize on deep passes, play action, screens, or any other situations where the goal is to gain a lot of yards. This way, players will operate on more linear paths and changes of direction are reduced.

If monitoring players with sport science technology, staff members should see the highest aerobic loads (like sustained heart rate elevation) and the most distance covered in the high volume, high density session, while accepting that movement speeds might be lower due to reduced recovery time between plays. The high-volume, high-density day is followed by the high-speed session, where volume and density are low, and intensity is high.

8.3 Intensity Exposure

Intensity really refers to how closely a practice achieves a game-like flow and how fast the players operate. High-intensity sessions often require frequent breaks (even if they are short) so they are often low density. In addition, high-intensity work goes together with high-collision, although the high-speed session later in the week will feature high-intensity with low-collision for purposes of recovery. It's impossible to sustain high intensity for very long due to nervous system demands, so the impact of such days is associated with low volume.

Let's clarify here to avoid confusion. High-volume practice days might certainly *feel* intense, where players are out of breath and feeling fatigued, but the key lies in the nervous system. A high-volume, high-density practice purposely builds fatigue into the format. When players are operating in a state of fatigue, they cannot move as fast as when they are fresh (by definition), so the intensity must drop. Therefore, they will not be operating at the upper limits of their power output and will instead be training their endurance qualities and aerobic systems.

We must understand the difference between fatigue
from intensity and fatigue from volume.

In the morphocycle, a high-intensity practice is one that features execution with as much focus as possible, high player speeds, and the option of collision with padded practices. This means that, as much as possible, offensive units should aim to get first downs and touchdowns and defensive units should aim to prevent first downs, prevent scoring, and cause turnovers. The volume will be reduced, so players should compete at a high level. To naturally build low-density into the practice, repetitions per series are lower in these sessions.

High-intensity days require a fair amount of rest intervals so players can maintain their physical outputs and sustain their focus for the tasks at hand. By keeping volume and density lower, the training effect is ensured, and the stress load is kept down. On high-collision days, smaller spaces and short-field situations can be emphasized to keep intensity high while reducing the magnitude of each collision, allowing players to experience more collision with less risk.

8.4   Density Exposure

In practice, density refers to how many breaks there are within each practice period. If the practice is high intensity, then density must be low to allow enough rest time to keep the players operating with great outputs and focus. But when seeking to improve endurance qualities, high-volume pairs well with high-density.

High-density sessions feature a higher overall load on the muscles and challenge the cardiorespiratory system as well. However, the load on the nervous system will be less and aerobic processes can help further stimulate nervous system recovery from a high-intensity session the day before.

8.5   Collision Exposure

In football, days that are high collision involve quite a bit of work with full pads on, possibly engaging in live situations and the use of tackling circuits. The higher injury risk associated with high-collision days requires lower volume and longer recovery times. These sessions are also typically broken up with plenty of rest and/or active recovery intermissions to keep density low.

High-collision days expose the muscles to high loading, but for a short time. That's why it makes sense to put high-intensity and high-collision exposure into the same practice day. Consider the catch phase of a power clean and how the players must sustain a lot of force but do so quickly.

Similarly, a tackler must run through a ball carrier with a lot of force but do so explosively. In addition, placing the high-intensity, high-collision practice earlier in the week exposes players to collision and still allows enough time for recovery by game day.

8.6   Sequencing the Stimuli

In terms of programming, the goal is to emphasize & de-emphasize each body system throughout the morphocycle so that each is rejuvenated and ready to perform at a high level on game day. In football, strength and power are paramount. This means that it's best to train these elements early in the week so that the affected body systems have as long as possible to recharge before they're called to action on game day.

Endurance training doesn't take as long to recover from, and endurance doesn't degenerate as quickly as strength and power. Speed is somewhere in between. In our experience, it can be useful to stress speed early in the weekly cycle and then top it up with lower volume as the week progresses using a practice day where high-speed is emphasized.

8.7   The Answers Lie in House

Throughout this section, many discussion points have been covered on organizing the weekly training elements throughout the football season to keep players performing at a high level. Some thoughts have been given as to how and why the morphocycle might be organized in certain ways and greater detail, sample routines and actionable information will be provided in the upcoming volumes of this series. However, no one can claim to have all the answers.

Ultimately, the way a team organizes its program will be based on what it deems appropriate, based on a collective effort to find the answers in-house. Open communication, transparency, attention to detail, and mindfulness are at the forefront of achieving sustainable success.

9 Using Games to Prepare for Games

The previous section shed some light on organizing in-season preparation. In this section, we will present a concept in relation to offseason preparation and how teams might use game-based activities to continue teaching the Game Model to players.

The great irony of football is that many of the players in the NFL developed their athleticism not with specialist coaches or highly-trained strength and speed experts, but with exposure to multiple sports/activities and free-play with their friends on back streets, uneven grass parks, or in their back yards. Only later in their teenage years are these skills brought to fruition in competitive high school sports.

Street versions of different games allow for children to improvise, perceive, and learn how to perform different actions and experience their associated consequences. This is a similar goal of physical education with young children: using different games with minimal rules and regulations and keeping participation fun and enjoyable. Such activities encourage creativity when it comes to scoring a goal, making a pass, or getting around an opponent.

The ability to anticipate and react to environmental stimuli is fundamental to all team sport players. Awareness, vison and reaction are skills players must maintain and develop beyond just practicing and playing a highly structured sport like football. Just as with children, different games can be used to accomplish this aim with older players, exposing them to a form of physical education all year.

As it currently stands, the NCAA and the Collective Bargaining Agreement (CBA) in the NFL have introduced time and training restrictions by which coaches must abide. In this reality, one primary aim is not necessarily to maximize training volume, but to optimize the time available with players.

With these restrictions in place, it is understood that players cannot simply practice football all year long. This would likely lead to physical and mental burn out, as evidenced by other team sport players that maintain a rigid practice structure throughout the entire year. But this does not mean players can't use other games to emphasize the same Game Model principles as football. In fact, the correct use of games in preparing players for performance can improve the synergy between perception and action, physically prepare players for activities they will be performing in practice, and help players avoid injury.

Perhaps most importantly, games are fun. Yes, fun and enjoyment are allowed. Remember, players started playing football for fun and enjoyment, so introducing games for conditioning keeps them focused while delivering a 'player experience' they will respond to.

9.1   From Perception to Action

Keeping true to the primary emphasis of this book, we believe that exposing players to small doses of game play throughout the offseason gives them the best opportunity to continue enhancing skill acquisition as well as prepare their bodies to better handle the stresses of organized practices and games. Inevitably, this process also involves the psychological coactive.

In the chaos of any game, players will continually and repeatedly go through the perception-action cycle. Players will have to observe their surroundings, orient themselves appropriately, decide how to respond to what they are seeing, and physically perform the decided action. This process is largely subconscious and based on previously formed habits.

In truth, the only way to help our players improve their OODA loop is to expose them to situations in which perception leads to action. Running around cones or through agility ladders does not feature much by way of perception. These activities are completely pre-determined, whereas perception-based activities will (by default) change from repetition to repetition. Information will guide the movement solution, just as it would in sport.

Various games and activities can be used to expose players to similar tactical situations requiring the same technical execution so that their inherent game play ability is enhanced while simultaneously exposing them to physical stressors needed for positive adaptation.

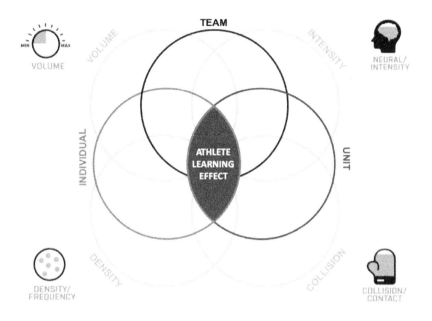

9.1.1   Facilitating Decision-Making

The way players perceive what's going on around them and anticipate what's going to happen next guides the skill they choose to execute. A sound comprehension of the Game Model gives players the freedom to make decisions, but also guides them into good decisions through repetition in training and practice.

The principles instilled and reinforced with the use of training games can better contextualize each situation that unfolds during a game and aid players' decision-making. Such principles improve individual decisions within the context of a team environment and overarching group goals.

It takes half a second or less for players to observe what's going on around them, select the best skill for the situation, and put it into action. This incredibly brief time frame shows that there is little (if any) time to think consciously about the best way to proceed. Decision-making is largely instinctual.

By incorporating training games, players can learn to better anticipate what's going to happen next in the events unfolding around them, reducing the time it takes to assess and act to a fifth of a second or less. This time reduction from anticipation to action comes from the experience of already being exposed to a similar situation in the past.

The goal is to create experiences that allow players to form positive habits so that they can react without thinking and be effective in a game setting.

9.2   The Physical Benefits of Training Games

It's hard to physically prepare players for the stresses of sport because isolating reasons for injuries is almost impossible. Injuries are multi-factorial and highly complex.

Take hamstring strains for example. One solution is to have players perform strengthening exercises for the hamstrings in hopes of diminishing the possibility of rupture. Or, maybe the player is not sprinting with biomechanically-sound technique, exposing his posterior chain to excessive and damaging amounts of force; so, he is coached to sprint more efficiently to reduce this strain.

These approaches may certainly be of help and should not be discouraged. However, despite interventions of strengthening muscles or improving biomechanics, multiple hamstring strains occur across multiple sports every year. The search for answers continues.

Many of the non-contact injuries in team sports are likely a result of players being unable to cope with chaos. No matter how well-prepared a player might be following training with sprints, jumps, or "perfect" lifting technique, these approaches will never fully prepare his mind and body for what really happens on the field.

The game is a wonderful blend of predictable and unpredictable factors. A player may already know what his opponent will *try* to do based on his preparation process. He may know the laws of the game and may understand the Game Model. But he can never be certain of what will *actually* happen in the moment. He just never knows what he will see or what actions he will have to take.

Think of any time you have ever tried to perform a skill you've never done before. Remember how awkward it was? Remember how rigid your body became as your brain tried its hardest to figure out what to do? When players are faced with situations that they can't handle, they get locked up, can't move, and stumble around. This is a highly injurious environment.

No matter how strong, powerful, or fast athletes become, if they encounter conflict exceeding what they can comfortably solve, their bodies will freeze and there will be no way to move efficiently or effectively. Their muscles will not fire in any synchronized manner, their tissues will tighten up, their minds will be stressed, and their internal environment will be sounding all kinds of alarms. If they are never trained to combine their actions with what they perceive, then they will always be at risk of injury when dealing with excessive chaos and conflict.

Training with games and abiding by monitored and progressive intensity and volume, it is possible to help players find the intricate balance between perception and action. In other words, the games get them comfortable being uncomfortable. It's less about perfecting specific movement patterns and more about learning when to use certain actions based on what's being perceived in the game. Effective actions will lead to effective outcomes, and training games set the stage for such effective actions.

Effective actions lead to effective outcomes.

While playing games, players' body structures will be exposed to similar stresses as those imposed in a sport, but the stress can be introduced in an organized, progressive manner to account for the total stress load. Moving through ladders and cutting around cones will never be enough to prepare players for the complexity of performing actions in a game-based environment. Conversely, using games in training will expose players to all the movements found in sport, but do so while enhancing the perception-action cycle.

9.3 Match Up Games

Games that feature very small numbers of players (i.e. one-on-one, two-on-two) we refer to as match up games simply due to their nature. We prefer to use the word "games" rather than "drills" because these activities incorporate the perception-action cycle in a way that resembles the game on a very small scale. These activities are competitive, with a definite winner and loser, making them game-like as opposed to going through rote-repetition movement.

For match up games, players will face off against each other in some sort of brief, high-intensity activity that mirrors a game situation - i.e. open field tagging to improve tackling pursuit, some form of man coverage like staying with a potential receiver, or trying to block a player from reaching a destination. Players will compete and then separate after the cessation of the activity so that another set of players can come together and compete.

A work-to-rest ratio of at least 1:5 – preferably upwards of 1:10 – is suitable to keep the activities alactic, allowing the performance to have maximum intensity and focus. This means that if two players compete for five seconds, they would then be given at least twenty-five to fifty seconds before another repetition.

This can easily be manipulated by staggering players into lines of certain numbers so that the rest times occur naturally as they cycle through their lines. For example, to accomplish a work-to-rest ratio of 1:5, a coach would set up players in lines of six, so that after one player goes another five will rotate through before he is up again.

Flags, flag belts, and evasion belts are very simple and effective forms of equipment for match-up games. Open field tackling situations can require pursuers to pull a flag off the hip of an evading player. Man-coverage situations can utilize evasion belts where one player tries to create separation and rupture the belt while the other tries to stay with him. Coaches can also use pop-up bags or some other forms of equipment as aiming points for players to touch, like in a game called "protect the pin" where a rusher attempts to get by a blocker and touch an object within an allotted time period.

Match up games are part of the backbone of sport - the most intense, focused game actions always occur in small number match ups. The ability to make opponents miss in the open field or stay with an opponent in coverage are paramount skills to sport success.

It's also an opportunity for a team's best talent to consistently face-off and make each other better while using reduced field spaces so that injury risk is minimized.

For these reasons, we advocate for keeping match up games present in controlled volumes all year long.

9.3.1   Classifying Match Up Games

Sport performance coaches Nick DiMarco and Jordan Nieuwsma have devised a simple classification system for breaking up match-up games. The broad classifications for these games are:

1. Chase Games
2. Mirror Games
3. Dodge Games
4. Score Games

Chase Games

These match up games feature one player attempting to chase down another. The simplest example of a Chase Game is the basic cat & mouse activity in which two players align either facing each other or away from each other, and the "mouse" moves away from the "cat" who must attempt to chase and catch it.

Variations can be used to change the starting positions or the degrees of freedom for the "mouse" in terms of which areas of the field are safe to run to. Generally, the game is decided by whether the "cat" was able to catch the "mouse."

Mirror Games

These match up games feature activities where one player must attempt to stay with another for a given duration of time. Though like a Chase Game, Mirror Games differ in that there is no sense of catching another player. The goal is simply to maintain position in staying with the opponent. One player is trying to create space through separation while the other tries to constrain space by mirroring the activity of the opponent.

Dodge Games

These match up games put players in positions to find gaps and space in the environment. Typically, one player runs towards a group of two to four opponents stacked in a line. As the running player approaches the line, the opponents scatter and take up areas of the field at which point the running player must visually scan for an open space and move through the gap.

Complexity can be increased by adding more players, having the running player catch a ball before scanning the field, or any other constraints a coach can think of adding.

Score Games

These match up games are based on basic evasion and making an opponent miss in the open field. These are essentially open field tag games where one player attempts to avoid being tagged and reach the other side of the playing area to "score."

Score Games are as up-front as it gets in terms of finding space or taking space away when a lot of field space exists. Complexity can be increased by adding more players, staggering players like one scoring player versus two defenders, or having one or both players start the drill "blind" where they won't know the location of the opponent until they turn around and find him.

9.4 Multi-Player Games

Multi-player games would be characteristic of physical education games that feature moderate numbers of players (i.e. 3v3 or 5v5). To keep players health and skill development in mind, it is not advisable to throw them into highly complex game situations at the start of the off-season. Instead, a plan can be formulated for gradually increasing the complexity of games, so there is a seamless transition into the start of true sport practice. Below is a basic three-stage progression for increasing multi-player game complexity:

1. Formation-Focused Games
2. Simple Invasion Games
3. Small-Sided Games

Formation-focused games will limit the amount of total movement by players while starting to introduce the Game Principles. In these games, there will not be any aspect of territory invasion. Instead, the emphasis will be on successfully passing a ball or other sport object, keeping a sport object off the ground, or wall/net games consisting of volleying a ball or other sport object.

These games have lower overall complexity with reduced movement ranges (keeping stress to a minimum) but they challenge players to learn aspects of structure/formation, ball circulation, player movement, and sequencing/timing of actions between teammates and opponents.

To reduce complexity in this initial stage, keep the number of players in each game relatively small, such as three-versus-three (3v3). Coaches can also stagger the number of players if wanting to challenge the offensive or defensive side of the ball, such as 2v3 or 3v5.

A trendy game that is formation-focused is Danney Ball, or Medicine Ball Volleyball, where players spread out like they would for standard volleyball. But, instead of striking a standard ball, they throw a weighted medicine ball (typically 6-12 pounds in weight) back and forth over a net. Rules can be varied in terms of whether the players can volley to each other on the same side or take a step before throwing the ball back. Performance coaches like Joe DeFranco have used this game with great buy-in from NFL players.

Another example of a formation-focused game is "keep the ball." Here, the object of the game is very simple:

- Two teams face off against each other within a defined boundary (i.e. 20yd x 20yd).
- The team in possession of the ball must attempt to make successful passes to teammates while the other team attempts to defend the ball by deflecting it or intercepting it.
- Points are assigned for number of successful passes, such as one point for three successful passes and two points for five successful passes.

- If five passes are completed or the defending team deflects or intercepts the ball, then there is a change in possession.
- If a pass is dropped or incomplete, but not touched by a defender, then the team in possession keeps possession and starts over from zero.
- The player holding the ball cannot move with his legs, but his teammates may run around the space and try to get open. Defenders must give the player in possession of the ball a three-foot cushion while he looks to complete a pass.
- The game play carries on for a defined time period and the team with the most points wins.

Note:
See Level II for the detailed explanation of using game variables for team sport development

9.4.2   Simple Invasion Games

Once game play has been introduced into the offseason with formation-focused games, games can progress into using simple invasion games. Now territories (i.e. end zones) are incorporated in order to score. Games can progress slowly from formation-focused games by manipulating certain rules, like limiting the ball carrier to a certain number of steps before the ball must be passed.

A good example of an introductory simple invasion game would be variations of ultimate frisbee. The game does not have to be played with a frisbee, but we can maintain similar rules. The offensive and defensive players may move freely around the playing space but the player in possession of the ball is limited to a small number of steps before having to pass. Again, in this stage it's better to keep player numbers on the lower end, like 3v3 or 5v5. Complexity will naturally rise with the change in game format.

9.4.3   Small-Sided Games

The final stage of the game progression is the use of small-sided games (SSGs). Up to this point, aspects of team-oriented game play have slowly been introduced with formation-focused games and simple invasion games. For SSGs, the idea is to really start letting players find their competitive edge against rising complexity, faster-flowing movement and decision-making.

With more degrees of freedom comes more complexity, focus, and intensity. Larger field spaces can be used (i.e. 30yd x 20yd) and players will be forced to find order amongst all the chaos. Again, it helps to use relatively simple games rules and allow players to self-organize and find their own solutions. The primary aim is to enforce the rules of the game, not give answers.

As a quick aside, coaches must be cautious and enforce the "play" aspect, reminding players that they may compete at a high intensity but not get carried away and act irrationally or dangerously. All these games should be conducted in a safe manner with great sportsmanship.

Players can be held accountable for penalties or going outside of the game rules. If players start to show signs of hot-headedness or putting other players at physical risk, they may be ejected and "punished" by having to perform more traditional, monotonous forms of conditioning like shuttle runs, or repeat 110-yard runs.

In free-flowing invasion games, players can move as much as they want, with or without the ball. A great example of this kind of game is "Agility Ball," which is really a modified version of rugby. Sport performance coaches Nick DiMarco and Jordan Nieuwsma have used this game with football players during offseason periods with very positive feedback and engagement.

Here are the basic rules for a game of Agility Ball:

- Each team begins at their respective end zones and a "roll off" occurs where one team rolls the ball to the other team to initiate play.
- Only lateral and backwards passing are allowed by the offensive team while advancing the ball.
- The goal is to successfully cross into the opposing end zone, which leads to a point, while avoiding being tagged. This is accomplished by evading defenders and completing passes to create space.
- The defensive players attempt to tag the player in possession of the ball. Six touches are allowed before the ball changes possession When a defensive player tags a ball carrier, he will yell out "touch!"
- If a ball carrier is tagged, he must stop in place and pass to a teammate within three seconds before he can move again. The defensive players must allow three feet of space for the ball carrier to pass the ball back into play.
- Change of possession occurs after six touches, after a score, if the ball hits the ground, if the ball carrier steps out of bounds, or if the ball is intercepted.
- No contact is allowed, and the players may not set picks for their teammates.
- After scoring occurs, each team aligns back at their end zone and the scoring team rolls the ball to the other team to start a new drive.
- The team with the most points at the end of play is the winner.

9.4.4   The Basis for All Game Intelligence

Training using games with fun and minimal instruction, players will figure out how to communicate verbally and non-verbally, as is required in any sports game. The basis for all game intelligence can be prepared in this simple game format. This is the foundation for all team invasion sports.

Players will soon start to show signs of natural game intelligence by staggering their runs to an appropriate tempo, matching up with players of similar ability, self-organizing their formations, gaining confidence by spreading the ball to multiple carriers, and starting to improvise their own movement solutions - all without any specific direction from coaches. This is one of our primary goals – developing habitual game intelligence.

9.4.5   Manipulating Game Rules for Different Training Effects

Within the framework of the morphocycle, coaches can structure games so that they may result in energy system-specific preparation. For example, in terms of rules and flow, one may use the exact same game to develop anaerobic capacity or aerobic capacity. The differences would lie in the play duration, breaks between rounds, size of the playing area, and number of players in the game to determine which energy pathway is emphasized.

Just like volume, intensity, density, and collision, each of the energy systems is always present in every game-based session, but one will be dominant depending on the nature of the work. The energy system emphasized for the day must be aligned with the morphocycle design and depend on the physical focus of the day. This will ensure a satisfactory stimulus to produce adaptation without compromising game deliverables.

When constructing the player experience, it's important to bear in mind some important aspects of training. As much as possible, coaches want to use games to create the experience, not drills. Drills are best used when a learning experience is in its very early stages or there's no possible way to recreate the experience in a training game.

For example, it's almost impossible for a player to hit his true maximum speed while playing small-sided games, so the use of speed drills is necessary to provide the player with a maximum speed experience to push his speed reserve threshold further, giving him potential to play faster when needed.

Here are some important considerations when designing games:

Central Nervous System and Learning Fatigue

It's not just physical activity that tires out the CNS but also cognitive load.

Game Complexity

The intensity of the players' concentration is directly related to how simple or complex the tasks are that they are trying to solve. The greater the complexity, the more concentration is required.

The more rules there are, the more difficult it is for players to focus and get to the intended learning outcome. Therefore, simplicity is often the best way forward when creating training games.

Number of Players

In training games, the number of players on each team is directly related to the variables of decision-making. The greater the number of players, the higher the complexity of the principles.

Playing Space

The speed of each player's decision-making correlates with the size of the space available. This also impacts physiology, as smaller spaces require players to change direction more sharply and frequently, leading to more eccentric muscle contractions and collision impacts.

Larger field spaces should be used primarily for development of aerobic fitness due to less lateral movement. For adaptation purposes and to minimize injury risk, the size of the playing area should not change by more than 20 percent when progressing games.

Team Selection

Usually teams are best split up evenly by fitness and position. However, teams can be divided between fit and unfit players so that the unfit players need to work harder and can improve their fitness.

Concurrent or Intermittent Timing

During games in which there are shorter periods of work, there is an increase in the distance spent at higher speeds, given that players are giving full effort. Games of longer work duration will result in higher perceived rates of exertion by the players involved, as well as higher average maximum heart rate percentages, indicating a greater endurance load.

However, games that appear continuous by design will always feature natural intermittent movement intensities as players will alternate between running, jogging, walking, and standing depending on the events of the game.

Change Field Size

Field A
Less lateral movement, more distance covered, ideal for game speed or aerobic development

Field B
More change of direction, greater eccentric stress, faster decision-making, ideal for game power & strength

Energy systems developed by manipulating work-to-rest ratios (1:1, 1:3, 1:5)

Note:
See
Level
II for
the

detailed explanation of using game variables for team sport development

9.4.6   General Guidelines for Training Games

Here are some universal guidelines when incorporating games into the team training sessions:

1. Keep work blocks between 1-4 minutes duration to keep focus and intensity high.
2. Ensure that players are moving at a competitive pace. If plodding sets in, there is need to intervene. Lack of focus and effort will only reinforce bad game habits and means that player work rates are dropping off.
3. Collision must be limited for reasons of safety. If players become too aggressive, coaches must intervene. Games should be competitive and fun but not put players at risk of contact injuries. Aspects of collision may be trained using other means like plyometrics or Olympic weightlifting.
4. Coaching cues should be limited as much as possible, likely coming in the form of verbal encouragement to help prevent players from hiding. Some players tend to sit back and avoid working hard in the organized chaos of games, which must be avoided for proper development.
5. Ensure that explosive, power-based movements continue through the whole duration of the work block. Games are competitive and can be intense due to the combination of high focus and high effort. Proper rest periods must be used to maintain quality of work and explosiveness. Coaches can expect some fatigue to set in with aerobic-based games, but movement output should not drop off too drastically.
6. Reduce the risk of non-contact injury by conducting games in smaller playing spaces before moving to bigger playing spaces, especially if the players are going to perform weight training during the same morning. Our game progression model accounts for this.
7. Rest periods may become shorter as the players become more acclimated to the use of games and as the competitive season approaches. This occurs over the course of weeks to months to help build functional capacity.
8. The most important thing in all training games is to maintain the intensity of action. This means full incorporation of the four-coactives, not just high physical intensity. Look for explosive movements, problem-solving, team communication, and high motivation.

Many offseason training programs are intelligently designed and based on sound exercise science principles that have stood the test of time. There are great efforts being taken around the world to find the most efficient ways to manipulate physiology and capitalize on performance gains.

However, in our opinion, many programs are lacking attention towards the pedagogical elements of team sport game play. That is, coaches tend to put a major emphasis on physiology and exercise science while ignoring the technical and tactical aspects of skill acquisition as they relate to performing in the context of sports games.

The following table shows an example of how games might fit in an offseason training week in conjunction with other forms of physical preparation:

Sample College Football Off-Season Game Development

Coaches allowed 8 hours/week with players + option of player-led captain's practices

	Day 1 Activation	Day 2 Strength	Day 3 Endurance	Day 4 Speed	Day 5 Active Recovery	Day 6 Game Day	Day 7 Off Day
Game Emphasis	Chase Alactic Games	Dodge/Score Alactic Games	Multi-Player Anaerobic or Aerobic Games	Mirror Alactic Games	Captain's Practice	Multi-Player Competitive Games	
Physical Emphasis	Activation, Potentiation	High-Intensity, High-Collision	High-Volume, High-Density	High-Speed	Active Recovery	Execution & Competition	
Sample Volume of Game Play	8-12 total repetitions	8-12 total repetitions	2-4 series x 2-4 mins of play	8-12 total repetitions	60 mins – no coaches, player-led	6-8 series x 4 mins of play	
Sample Field Size (WxL)	10yd x 10yd 15yd x 15yd 5yd x 15yd	10yd x 10yd 15yd x 15yd 5yd x 15yd	10yd x 20yd 20yd x 30yd	10yd x 10yd 15yd x 15yd 5yd x 15yd	Reduced spaces	30yd x 50yd	
Sample Player Numbers	1v1, 2v2, 1v2, 1v3, 2v3	1v1, 2v2, 1v2, 1v3, 2v3	3v3, 5v5, 2v3, 3v5	1v1, 2v2, 1v2, 1v3, 2v3	Player-led 7v7	7v7	
Sample Complimentary Physical Preparation	CNS Activation	High Force	Work Capacity	High Velocity	Active Recovery	Games Only	Off
	Acceleration/Power Capacity Complexes Upper Body Strength Hypertrophy	Acceleration Development (10-30yds) Explosive Jumps & Throws Olympic Lifts / Loaded Power Lower Body Strength	Tempo Running/ General Aerobic Work Upper Body Strength Endurance Hypertrophy	Speed Development (20+ yds) Elastic Power & Plyometrics Explosive Jumps/ Throws Lower Body Strength	Soft Tissue & Mobility Work General Physical Circuits Personal Recovery Strategies		
Coach-Led Session Duration	1 hour	2 hours	2 hours	1.5 hours	30 mins	1 hour	

We believe there is a positive shift that occurs in player development when players are exposed to training games throughout the year. Why are strength and conditioning coaches paid so much at the highest levels of football? The common answer is because they spend the most time with the players.

The head coach and football assistant coaches are limited in their access to the players in the offseason, but the strength staff has full access. We believe that this is exactly the reason why it is a responsibility of the strength and conditioning staff to learn the tactical and technical aspects of their head coach's plan for the team.

We believe that a team's greatest performance edge is the power of communication. If the strength staff can come together with the coaching staff and learn about how they teach certain skills, why they call certain plays, and what the players will be asked to do once the season comes around, then the offseason can be a wonderful opportunity to design drills and games to continue developing these principles while abiding by the rules and regulations.

10 Winning and Leadership

10.1 The Six Laws of Winning

One of the most important sets of principles Fergus has adapted from those outlined by the U.S. Army Special Operations Command are the truths that winning teams need to accept. If one had to boil down the management of any sports team to a few simple points, these are what would come up.

10.1.1 The Law of Knowledge

Coaches and managers will instantly have a greater chance of success if they know the game and understand the people who play and coach it. If there is no basic understanding of what is being done and what needs to be done, then there cannot be success. If coaches and managers do not possess an understanding of human nature or the ability to connect with people and players on a deeper level, then organizations cannot be successful.

It's not a question of having knowledge of the game *or* people … one must have both. Veteran coaches often joke with newly hired, first time head coaches and say, "At this point, you know as much about the game as you will ever know … your focus now turns to knowing how to manage people."

10.1.2 The Law of Human Superiority

Ultimately, successful teams depend on people. Human beings are more important than any technology or analytics program. For all the hype about new technology and the millions that are spent on all the latest and supposedly greatest equipment, sport is still, at its core, a people business and always will be.

Actual human beings are always the number one asset, not state-of-the-art stadiums or fancy training facilities. Those things are nice and have a purpose, but the bulk of a team's investment must be on finding ways to attain the right people: managers, coaches, players, and supportive staff members.

The best facilities and best equipment are useless unless the right personnel are available to wield it all. Further, no combination of technology or equipment is perfect, so people are relied upon to pick up the slack. Teams can spend money on coaching management applications, scouting software, and all the rest, but one absolutely must invest the most time and energy in the workability, health and well-being of players, coaches, and staff.

> *"I had a chance to ask all these coaches, 'What are you doing out with these GPSes? What are you getting out of that? And I hear a lot of the guys saying, 'Not much.' I hear that. Then I go another place, and they're using it, and they're spending a fortune on it. They got sleep bracelets, they got time chambers, they got the goggles, the quarterbacks are watching 3D vision.*
>
> *"You can buy all that, spend millions of dollars, and turn this into whatever you want. And we have. We have as good a technology as anyone. But what can you use? I ticked a lot of people off for some reason when I said, 'We're gonna get back to the nuts and bolts of football,' because I have seen a lot of the gimmicks and gadgets not really be beneficial. Is it helping them get better?"* [CIX]
>
> -Jon Gruden

Just as players are expected to know their roles and work together in a synchronized way during a game, team managers should have the same expectations for coaches and staff in their jobs. If a manager and/or head coach encourages everyone to try to better understand their colleagues' needs, objectives, and challenges, then all in-person interactions will be exponentially more respectful and professional.

10.1.3   The Law of Intensity and Quality
Intensity and quality always trump volume and quantity. In the book *Team of Teams: New Rules of Engagement for a Complex World,* General Stanley McChrystal explains the approach put into action when the U.S. military faced warfare with Al

Qaeda. He outlines how the military had to rely on small, highly trained, and self-reliant groups that could be deployed anywhere at a moment's notice.

The same principle holds true for how a sports team operates the organizational system, from putting a staff together to how the Game Plan is formulated. It seems better to have a small, tight-knit group of focused, experienced, and committed people than a massive coaching and back-office staff that doesn't fully commit to the ideals of the team and head coach.

Intensity and quality also carry over into practice sessions and strength and conditioning workouts. It's easy to chase numbers and run players into the ground. But what good is that? If coaches can find ways to be minimalists in their volume while being maximalists in their results, then quality stays high and room is left for more learning and growing.

10.1.4   The Law of Individual Contribution

Developing winners takes time and there are no shortcuts. Sustainable, championship-oriented organizations don't just spring to life overnight. It's imperative that leaders and staff acknowledge the hard work of everyone at every level of the organization and make it a point to highlight their achievements. If leaders don't care for and respect good people, the good people will soon find another organization that does.

10.1.5   The Law of Preparation

To be a successful team, the team must prepare for crises before they happen and be ready when chaos unfolds. Once problems manifest themselves, it's far too late to come up with an action plan for dealing with them. The plan must already exist and be (at a minimum) tested in practice. This is one of the reasons why a weekly walk-through or talk-through the day before a game is an essential discipline.

If head coaches can find ways to prepare players and assistant coaches for as many eventualities as can be contrived, not only will anxiety be reduced but the coaching staff will have strategized for everything that can (and probably will) go wrong, so there's a planned response for any eventuality. Good teams expect the unexpected and prepare for it to the best of their ability.

Let's be real though. Once the game kicks off and the ball is in play, emergencies will undoubtedly occur. If a starting player is injured, coaches must ensure the potential replacement is adequately prepared (in all four coactives) so that he can enter the game and perform effectively. If the team has practiced in a way that allows for a deep bench of players who are prepared and ready to go at a moment's notice, it is much easier to weather the injury storm that tends to bedevil every team at some point in the season.

In the same way, if there is a system in place that everyone understands, then assistant coaches can take over practices and games if the head coach is unable to perform his duties because of illness, a family emergency, or some other unexpected event. The most successful teams are not the biggest or the strongest, but those that can best adapt to the stresses and challenges they face.

10.1.6   The Law of Support

Winners require outside support. The reality of the game is that no player or team can win independently. Dozens of support staff personnel contribute to a team's success. This includes those inside the organization – like the maintenance staff who keep the locker room clean, the cafeteria staff who prepare, serve, and clear away the food, and the equipment managers who make sure the kit is ready to go for each practice.

It also encompasses a lot of external people who often go unnoticed, such as the bus drivers who get the team to the stadium, the hotel staff who check in the team and get rooms ready, and the airline crews who serve in-flight drinks and meals. If all these support staff members suddenly disappeared or went on strike, the team would be unable to function.

The behind-the-scenes folks who do the "little things" needed to keep a team on track will put in extra effort for players and coaches who are courteous, respectful, and grateful to them. Conversely, they will not go out of their way to help those who treat them rudely and might even start underserving them when they next meet. Therefore, it's important that the head coach makes it clear to everyone that, whether at home or on the road, they must treat others with respect.

10.2 The Four Primary Principles of Winning Teams

These four primary principles are critical to successful leadership. These are the trends found amid successful organizations and with coaches that have "growth mindsets," meaning that they believe a team can always develop in its abilities. Success here extends beyond on-field performance. Success is also about establishing a sustainable culture that attracts, retains, and rewards the best people. It all starts with the head coach.

Sustainable winning is different from a one-off victory or a single successful season. With the right wind behind the sails, coaches can find a way to force their team to summon all its resources into a major effort to achieve something great during a rivalry game or tail-end of a long season. But sustaining success game after game, year after year, is far more difficult to achieve and a far scarier proposition for opponents.

10.2.1 Humility

Pride in the team and the jerseys worn is certainly something to encourage. Players and coaches should be proud to wear the team's emblem and uniform. But pride can be a dangerous value to encourage at times when it has the chance of promoting the idea of self-importance. Teams must always be careful of players or coaches that can be labeled as "me guys," meaning that they selfishly put their own pride above the success of the team.

Humility instead puts the focus on honor as achieved through a collective team effort. Humility is observant of the service of a team and a player's realization of his place relative to everyone else in the organization.

"It's awfully important to win with humility. It's also important to lose. I hate to lose worse than anyone, but if you never lose you won't know how to act. If you lose with humility, then you can come back."

– Paul "Bear" Bryant

Humility is at the core of every successful football team, from the head coach down. One of the reasons humble people continue to improve is that humility discourages complacency. If one is truly humble, then one knows that what has been achieved is not worth being arrogant about, and there is always a way to keep striving to do better. That's not to say that players and coaches can't be satisfied with a job well done. But it's important to put titles, championships, and other achievements in the context of a team's history.

Take Bill Belichick, for example. There is no excessive celebration or taunting of opponents by his teams; there's no lapsing into overconfidence or complacency. Despite all the Super Bowl wins, Belichick is committed to a cold, ruthless, almost mechanical pursuit of success.

Once a team leader – whether that leader is a coach or a player – becomes puffed up and prideful, the focus switches from the higher ideal to individual interests. Rather than put the team above all, an arrogant person will look to satisfy himself and succeed for his own glory. The "disease of me" takes precedence at the intended or unintended expense of other teammates and the whole group.

Therefore, players and coaches must endeavor to be anything but self-consumed and should continually demonstrate humility in all interactions with the team, the media, and fans. They must also make it a point to look for and snuff out pride and arrogance in the locker room before it can take root, particularly when a player is excelling, and the team is winning.

Humility is also demonstrated in gratitude. It's quick and easy to say, "thank you" or "I'm grateful for that," and while it might seem like a small thing, it can have significant positive results. By expressing gratitude, head coaches show that they know they can't go it alone, and they value the help that others continually provide. Humility allows perspective on both success and failure.

Humility allows a healthy sense of introspection that constantly keeps players and coaches aware of their achievements, their strengths, and their failures and weaknesses in totality. This healthy awareness is critical to continuous development and progression.

10.2.2 Hunger

Everyone wants something big, but most people don't want to put in the effort to obtain it. To be successful, teams must want something badly enough to pay the price. At the highest echelon of sport, there are many great players, talented coaches, and proficient specialists. Team members can only rise above their peers by approaching their craft with hunger and a ruthless pursuit of excellence. Great success means great self-sacrifice, self-discipline, and great self-denial, and few want to go through all that.

"Winning isn't everything but wanting to win is."

– Vince Lombardi

10.2.2.1 Accountability

Every successful coach and player are highly ambitious and goal oriented. It's the job of those around them to hold them accountable for directing this drive toward the greater goals of the group rather than to selfish ends. To reach the pinnacle of achievement, players must try to maximize their own gifts and hold everyone around them accountable for doing the same.

Those who are self-motivated won't need eyes on them to give their best—they will just do it, even with little supervision. For a successful organization, disciplined doers who can make decisions independently and act appropriately are needed.

10.2.2.2 Focus

Success in sport requires focus. In war, special operators must always keep the objective in mind, despite the chaos unfolding noisily around them. It's the same for a sport team, and team members must block out the potential distractions of media rumors, the roar of the crowd, and the weight of expectation.

Everyone must zero in on their specific role and do what it takes to execute. This encompasses seemingly routine activities, such as observation and scouting, as well as game-day performance.

10.2.3 Hard Work

No one gets out of this world alive. There is no sense in the coaching staff, players, or back-office personnel holding back anything for later. For a team to reach its potential and achieve its goals, everybody must remain dedicated to daily hard work. This isn't just the case while chasing the first championship; it's even more true after such an achievement. It's a cliché in sports that the hardest thing is winning back-to-back titles, but if you look at the numbers, it's also a fact. Only seven NFL franchises have claimed successive titles.

One of the reasons that teams might reach the pinnacle of a championship title one year and fall short the next is that in the absence of hunger, complacency develops. In contrast, dynasty-oriented teams don't set the goal of winning just one championship; they want to win as many as possible. Nick Saban and Dabo Swinney consistently find themselves in the college football playoffs every year because they never lose hunger or show signs of complacency. After a team has been victorious, the organization needs to continue to practice the same habits that earned this success in the first place to avoid the pitfalls of a one-and-done achievement. Hard work must be intrinsically motivated and driven by solid, repeatable habits if it's to be sustained day after day, season after season.

> *"The process is really what you have to do day in and day out to be successful, we try to define the standard that we want everybody to sort of work toward, adhere to, and do it on a consistent basis.*
>
> *And the things that I talked about before, being responsible for your own self-determination, having a positive attitude, having great work ethic, having discipline to be able to execute on a consistent basis, whatever it is you're trying to do, those are the things that we try to focus on, and we don't try to focus as much on the outcomes as we do on being all that you can be."* [xxv]
>
> *– Nick Saban*

10.2.3.1 Commitment

To work toward a greater goal over several years, the team must display an unwavering commitment to its aims and to each team member. Embodying commitment goes a long way with boosting team morale. Coaches can do their best not to demand attitudes and actions of players that they are unwilling to do themselves.

Charlie Strong reportedly does not hesitate to hop into the offseason workouts with his players and show them that he is there with them throughout the grind. This type of dedication carried over to the practice field as well, and Strong's players from his time at the University of Texas described him as being "really real." [xxvi]

Nobody wants to make sacrifices for a leader who just *tells* them to risk everything—they must be conditioned to follow the coach and strive for a higher ideal that's bigger and more important than themselves. It's not enough for players to commit completely in their own heads. Their commitment must be demonstrated at every game, every practice, and every team meeting. And this commitment starts with the head coach.

If players and assistants can see that their leader is all in, then they're far more likely to put everything on the line as well. Teams can buy or recruit star players, but they cannot buy loyalty; loyalty comes about only when there's a top-down commitment that's always evident.

> *"I just want them to know who we are. When a young man knows that you care about him, he'll do everything you ask of him."*
>
> *– Charlie Strong*

10.2.4 Honesty

Coaches must insist on brutal honesty at all levels. When people are honest with each other, everyone knows exactly where they stand, what is expected, and what others think of their performance. It's the same as when you ask a good friend for advice. You shouldn't just want affirmation but rather honesty and a fresh perspective that will help you make the best possible decision.

People are often loath to criticize players and coaches who have already been very successful. This can have the knock-on effect of making such people react poorly to honest appraisal because they're not used to it and may come to think that they're above criticism. However, the best of the best want peers to keep critiquing, because it provides extra motivation to push to new heights. It can also be helpful to have mentors and a small circle of close friends outside the organization to whom one periodically looks for honest evaluation.

> *"Leadership is a matter of having people look at you and gain confidence. . . If you're in control, they're in control."*
>
> —Tom Landry

When a head coach is honest with his assistants, back office staff, and players, it fosters trust throughout the organization. Trust helps create and sustain loyalty, dedication to one another, and adherence to a purpose that's greater than any individual goal or desire. When everyone is honest, the burden of trying to be something they're not and attempting to appear flawless is lifted.

Honesty and truthfulness also help a team improve because each person can critically assess his own strengths and weaknesses. Humility is a prerequisite for honesty because only when people are humble can they feel secure and can ask for, accept, and act on honest and constructive criticism. However, the single most important aspect of honesty is self-honesty. The ability to critically analyze one's own ability, strengths, and weaknesses is essential to creating a sustainable-winning organization.

11 Conclusion

As we outlined at the beginning of this book, sport is medium through which we prepare young people for life. We as coaches are fortunate to have the privilege to impact young people in so many ways daily. Players learn how to overcome trials, win and lose with honor, and accept the challenge of competition in the public arena of a game field.

This book is not the definitive resource for coaching sport. That book will probably never be written. Nonetheless, this resource introduces new concepts for you as the coach and player to explore, implement and improve with your team. We hope that it positively impacts, challenges, and helps you impact all those in your care.

Enjoy the journey.

12 Authors

Fergus Connolly

Fergus is one of the world's leading experts in performance.
Fergus Connolly has worked with leading CEO's, professional sports teams, elite special forces units and athletes around the world.

He is the author of "59 Lessons - Working with the World's Elite Coaches, Athletes & Special Forces" and "Game Changer - The Art of Sports Science," the first book to present a holistic philosophy for all team sports.

Dr. Connolly has been Director of Elite Performance for the San Francisco 49ers, Sports Science Director with the Welsh Rugby Union, and Performance & Operations Director for University of Michigan football.

Learn more at fergusconnolly.com

Cameron Josse

Cameron Josse is the Director of Sports Performance for DeFranco's Training Systems in East Rutherford, NJ.

Cameron has been working with DeFranco's Training Systems since 2013 and has quickly built up a resume working with a multitude of athletes in high school and collegiate sports, as well as professional athletes in the NFL, NHL, UFC, and WWE superstars.

Cameron earned his bachelor's degree in kinesiology while playing football at the University of Rhode Island and holds a master's degree in exercise science from William Paterson University.

13 Online Education

To Learn More …

https://fergusconnolly.thinkific.com/

https://fergusconnolly.thinkific.com/

14 Game Changer

Game Changer: The Art of Sports Science

In Game Changer, Fergus Connolly shows how to improve performance with evidence-based analysis and athlete-focused training. Through his unprecedented experiences with teams in professional football, basketball, rugby, soccer, Aussie Rules, and Gaelic football, as well as with elite military units, Connolly has discovered how to break down the common elements in all sports to their basic components so that each moment of any game can be better analyzed, whether you're a player or a coach.

Available on Amazon!

15 <u>Coming Soon</u>

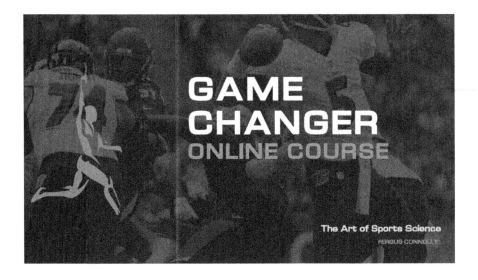

https://fergusconnolly.thinkific.com/

17 59 Lessons

59 Lessons: Working with the World's Greatest Coaches, Athletes, & Special Forces

In '59 Lessons' Fergus Connolly reveals the secrets learned first-hand from working with the world's greatest winners. Learn how the most successful coaches, athletes and special forces lead, manage and win in the most demanding environments. Find out how the best teams create winning cultures. Learn what makes great players truly special and how the best organizations use technology and people to create sustainable success.

This unique insight helps you understand how the world's elite prepare and win, from Premier League soccer, The NFL, NBA, Olympic Champions, International Rugby and worlds most secret Special Forces.

Available on Amazon!

18 Suggested Reading

- Essentials of Strength and Conditioning-3rd Edition by the National Strength and Conditioning Association
- Supertraining by Yuri Verkhoshansky and Dr Mel Siff
- Starting Strength by Mark Rippetoe and Jason Kelly
- Practical Programming for Strength Training by Mark Rippetoe and Andy Barker
- Science and Practice of Strength Training by Vladimir Zatsiorsky and William Kraemer
- Periodization 5th Edition by Tudor Bompa and G. Gregory Haff
- Coach's Strength Training Playbook by Joe Kenn
- Talent is Overrated: What Really Separates World-Class Performers from Everyone Else by Geofrey Colvin
- The Talent Code: Greatness isn't Born. It's Grown. Here's How by Daniel Coyle
- Triphasic Training by Cal Dietz & Ben Peterson
- Charlie Francis Training System by Charlie Francis
- Speed Trap by Charlie Francis
- New Functional Training for Sports by Michael Boyle
- 5/3/1 The Simplest and Most Effective Training System for Raw Strength by Jim Wendler
- CEO Strength Coach by Ron McKeefrey
- Explosive Strength Development for Jumping by Louie Simmons
- Westside Barbell Bench Press Manual by Louie Simmons
- Westside Barbell Squat and Deadlift Manual by Louie Simmons
- Westside Barbell Book of Methods by Louie Simmons
- Athletic Body in Balance by Gray Cook
- Strength and Power in Sport by Paavo V. Komi
- Low Back Disorders: Evidenced-Based Prevention and Rehabilitation by Stuart McGill
- Strength Training Anatomy by Frédéric Delavier
- Movement by Gray Cook

- Principles and Practice of Resistance Training by Mike Stone, Meg Stone, William A. Sands
- The Stress of Life by Hans Seyle
- Flow in Sports by Mihaly Csikszentmihalyi
- Uncommon by Tony Dungy
- Think Like a Champion by Mike Shanahan
- You Win in the Locker Room First by Jon Gordon and Mike Smith
- Behave by Robert Sapolsky
- Why Zebras Don't Get Ulcers by Robert Sapolsky
- Strength Training & Coordination: An Integrative Approach by Frans Bosch
- What We Need is Speed by Henk Kraaijenhof
- Block Periodization by Vladimir Issurin
- Team of Teams: New Rules of Engagement for a Complex World by Gen. Stanley McChrystal
- Extreme Ownership by Jocko Willink & Leif Babin

19 <u>Notes</u>

i Nick Saban, Thinking Ahead, Builds a Faster Defense to Get Him There - The New York Times 1/6/17, 11'45

ii https://theramswire.usatoday.com/2018/06/26/nfl-los-angeles-rams-ranking-top-100-players-quotes-video/

iii https://www.therams.com/news/quotes-and-notes-9-13-mcvay-praises-gurley-s-instincts-and-versatility

iv http://www.stack.com/a/the-secret-to-alabama-footballs-success-the-hardest-practices-in-the-nation

v https://www.theringer.com/2016/9/9/16036650/chip-kelly-san-francisco-49ers-offense-f332f053870e#.hr4m2yk7

vi How the Patriots Stay Winning, The Ringer, https://theringer.com/nfl-playoffs-new-england-patriots-keys-to-sustained-success-bill-belichick-tom-brady-f6fcf1678061#.vokhmc4um

vii Alabama's Super-Scout on the Sideline Is Also the Head Coach - The New York Times 1/6/17

ix The Patriots' Ever-Adapting Offense Is Built to Endure - The Ringer 2/6/18

x http://profootballtalk.nbcsports.com/2017/05/15/bill-belichick-says-a-smaller-staff-is-a-better-staff/

xi Woelfle, Ouyang, Phanvijhitsiri, Johnson, The adaptive value of circadian clocks: an experimental assessment in cyanobacteria. Curr Biol. 2004 Aug 24;14(16):1481-6

xii Sean McVay says 'it can't be healthy' to coach in the NFL for a long time https://theramswire.usatoday.com/2018/07/23/nfl-los-angeles-rams-sean-mcvay-coaching-years-hbo-real-sports/

xiii http://www.profootballhof.com/players/kurt-warner/biography/

xiv Behind the scenes work triggered New England Patriots' defensive improvement 10/30/17, 08]05 http://www.nbcsports.com/boston/patriots/behind-scenes-work-triggered-patriots-defensive-improvement?amp

xv Progress in Motor Control: Bernstein's Traditions in Movement Studies, Bunker LK., J Athl Train. 1999 Jul-Sep; 34(3): 296-297

xvi "Boyd: The Fighter Pilot Who Changed the Art of War", R. Coram

xvii http://www.espn.com/blog/los-angeles-rams/post/_/id/39047/sean-mcvays-culture-resonates-with-rams-players

xviii No More Questions by David Fleming http://www.espn.com/espn/feature/story/_/id/17703210/new-england-patriots-coach-bill-belichick-greatest-enigma-sports

xix S&C for Sports Performance - Goodwin & Cleather

xx https://profootballtalk.nbcsports.com/2013/02/26/tyrann-mathieus-bench-press-may-call-his-work-ethic-into-question/

xxi High Performance Training for Sports - Gregory Dupont

xxii Alabama's Super-Scout on the Sideline Is Also the Head Coach - The New York Times 1/6/17 [xxiii] Rhea, M. R., Hunter, R. L., & Hunter, T. J. (2006). Competition Modeling Of American Football: Observational Data And Implications For High School, Collegiate, And Professional Player Conditioning. *Journal of Strength and Conditioning Research, 20*(1), 58-61. Retrieved from https://ezproxy.wpunj.edu/login?url=https://search-proquest-com.ezproxy.wpunj.edu/docview/213066665?accountid=15101) [2017 Pro Football Reference, LineUps.com, TeamRankings.com, FootballOutsiders.com

[xxiv] https://www.si.com/nfl/2018/08/13/jon-gruden-oakland-raiders-return-jaguars-jalen-ramsey-dante-fowler-fight-media-suspensions

[xxv] http://www.spongecoach.com/best-nick-saban-quotes/

[xxvi] https://sports.yahoo.com/blogs/ncaaf-dr-saturday/charlie-strong-won-t-allow-his-players-to-throw-up-the–hook–em-horns–yet-163814369.html

Printed in Great Britain
by Amazon